HELP! I TEACH YOUTH SUNDAY SCHOOL

Other Books in the HELP! Series

Help!

I Teach Youth
Sunday
School

brian foreman
bo prosser
david woody

SMYTH&HELWYS
PUBLISHING, INCORPORATED — MACON, GEORGIA

Smyth & Helwys Publishing, Inc.
6316 Peake Road
Macon, Georgia 31210-3960
1-800-747-3016
©2004 by Smyth & Helwys Publishing
All rights reserved.
Printed in the United States of America.

The paper used in this publication meets the minimum requirements of
American National Standard for Information Sciences—
Permanence of Paper for Printed Library Materials.
ANSI Z39.48–1984. (alk. paper)

Library of Congress Cataloging-in-Publication Data

Foreman, Brian, 1972–
Help! I teach youth Sunday school / by Brian Foreman, Bo Prosser
& David Woody.
p. cm.
Includes bibliographical references and indes
p. cm.
ISBN 1-57312-427.3 (pbk. : alk. paper)
1. Christian education—Teaching methods.
2. Sunday school teachers.
3. Church work with teenagers.
I. Prosser, Bo.
II. Woody, David, 1967-
III. Title.
BV1534.F62 2004
268'.433—dc22

2004001346

Contents

From Brian:
For those who shape me into what God
wants me to be . . . students, teachers, and friends
For colleagues who became family
For Denise, Brock, and Adria
You all make ministry worth it!

From Bo:
For those youth who challenged me and endured . . .
I'm proud of you!
For those youth teachers who helped me grow . . .
I'm thankful for you!
JKGBW . . . for keeping me young . . .
I love you tons!

From David:
To Emilie, Brooks, and Blair . . . my 3 girls . . .
for the love, the time and the support . . .
I love you!
For Eddie, Don, and Bo . . .
who helped shape me into who I am . . . thank you!
For the youth and youth teachers . . . for giving me the
opportunity to grow on the journey . . . thanks for sharing!

From the authors:
To Miss A, Bluize, Randy—the D.A.C.!
We love you!

Introduction

Bo Prosser tells a story of the first time he attended a training event for teaching youth. The speaker began, "Don't be afraid of teenagers. You must remember, they are just big kids with almost-adult bodies. You can *make* a teenager do just about anything you want them to do." "I walked out of the training," Bo remembers. "I was so angry with the speaker!"

Teenagers are special! We thrive off their energy and zest for life. They are not children. Even young adolescents have moved beyond childhood and are racing toward maturity. While they may act childish sometimes, they are no longer children. People who treat teens as "big kids" miss how special youth are.

Teenagers are experiencing changes. Certainly, their bodies are growing into adulthood, but most them struggle emotionally to understand their bodies, feelings, and actions. These are years of great change. Our job is to help teenagers understand some of what is happening in their lives and cope with the changes they face. People who see teens as people with "almost-adult" bodies miss how special youth are.

Certainly, teenagers can be "made" to do just about anything. But that doesn't make it right! Manipulative messages bombard our youth. Madison Avenue, sports teams, alcohol and tobacco companies, and countless other media target them. Their friends try to influence them. Even their parents sometimes try to manipulate them. Somebody must stand up for teens. They need an honest voice, a voice of integrity and trust. Those who would try to "make" teens do almost anything miss how special youth are.

Youth are a special group of people. Adolescence is a time of great energy and enthusiasm. The youth with whom we work need to hear mature voices of reason. Teens today are searching for role models who have integrity. They are not looking to be manipulated. They are looking for leadership.

Adolescent learners with whom we work are special too. Youth are eager to learn, eager to express, eager to create. This makes teaching teenagers easy. However, youth are also eager to interact with friends, eager to challenge boundaries, and eager to make their own way. This makes teaching teenagers challenging.

Adolescent development needs direction, not manipulation. Today's young people are street-savvy. They know when they are being manipulated. They know when someone makes false claims. They can see through a phony persona; they are not swayed by religious rhetoric.

Be "real" with your youth! Tom was a challenging youth learner. He was into the culture of his day. He came from an affluent family. He had everything a kid could want except an understanding of his faith. Tom and his youth minister spent many days together sharing about life. The minister tried to help him grasp some understanding about the importance of being a person of faith. Sometimes in this sharing Tom would fuss, sometimes he would curse (to see the youth minister's reaction), and sometimes he would make mature observations.

One day, Tom said to his youth minister, "Why can't more ministers be like you? Too many ministers cover up their lives with God-talk and unrealistic expectations. You are real! The kids at church know that we can talk to you about anything. We know you won't judge us or talk down to us. Why can't more ministers be real?"

Wow! Tom humbled his youth minister and teaches us all a valuable lesson. Youth want to see a real witness of faith. Youth want to know that we struggle just like they struggle. Youth also want to know that we survive, maybe even thrive, in and through our faith. They want to know how they can survive/thrive too.

Being real with youth means we guide their development, not script their lives. Being real with youth means we tell them honestly what we think while allowing them to form their own thoughts. Being real with youth means we share biblical truths with integrity instead of twisting Scripture to fit our motives. Being real with youth means we listen to their stories and not violate their trust in us. Being real with youth means we are their friends without reverting to our own adolescent behaviors.

Being real isn't easy, but Jesus gave us the model for being real! Jesus showed us how to be childlike without being childish. He showed us how to confront sin while loving sinners. He showed us how to teach with integrity and with loving challenges. Jesus showed us how to teach with stories and songs instead of a boring lecture prepared the night before. Jesus showed us how to teach with the needs of the learners in mind rather than dumping our agenda on our listeners. He showed us that true community could develop as teachers share honestly from their personal struggles. Jesus modeled for us how to grow in wisdom and stature and in favor with God and people. So must we!

In today's postmodern culture, youth are searching desperately for someone who will be open and honest. In today's market-driven society, youth need someone who will treat them like a friend, not a consumer. In today's frenzied lifestyles, youth hope beyond hope for someone to slow down and sit and share. In a world marked by virtual reality, youth urgently seek someone and something that is real.

Be ready for youth! For all the years of my ministry, my guiding mission/vision statement has been "People go where they know they've been prepared for and are cared for!" This statement is truer today than ever, especially when we focus on young people.

How many of us have sat through boring, one-dimensional, non-interactive Bible studies? These studies do little more than fulfill the obligation of the teaching assignment. We have in our possessions the good news about life, yet we treat this good news as if it were just another piece of information!

Every week, keep in mind that people go where they know they are prepared for and cared for. We'll have more to say about this later in the book, but understand that youth know whether or not you have prepared for them. They know if you care about them or not. You must do as much preparing and caring outside the classroom as you do inside the classroom. "Prepared for and cared for" will happen in the context of attending teenagers' sports games, school dramas, parades, and pageants. "Prepared for and cared for" means you understand some of their language, relate to some of their TV shows, know their favorite celebrities, listen to their music, and know their movies. Being ready for youth is more than simply "getting a lesson together."

Being ready isn't easy, but Jesus modeled "prepared for and cared for." He showed us how to be attentive by the way he shared with the woman at the well. He showed us how to be caring in the patient ways he dealt with the apostles. He modeled sensitivity to others as he brought Lazarus back from the grave. He modeled an awareness of physical needs as he fed the 5,000. Jesus modeled "prepared for and cared for" with everyone around him. So must we!

This generation is filled with high-tech gadgets; youth need high *touch* too. Today's youth know much more about technology than we do. "Prepared for and cared for" gives us the opportunity to be personal and relevant with teens in order to touch them with God's love.

Many of today's youth are characterized as "latchkey-kids," meaning they have basically helped to raise themselves. As they come to our churches, let us receive them with open arms. Let us reach out to these youth who have had to find community over the Internet, through cable television, and over cell phones. Let us be the reality of God's love in their world of ambiguity and anonymity.

Be responsive to your youth! When you are real and ready, young people will seek you out. They will come seeking answers to complex questions. They will come looking for truth amid confusing and conflicting solutions. Too many of them have been pushed aside as irrelevant. Too many of them have had unrealistic demands placed on them by a single parent. Too many of them feel neglected and lonely. They are testing to see if you will respond to them.

Their tests will come in the form of challenges to your faith. They want to know what you think about sexual activity. They want to know your ideas on the good and evil of money. They want to know how your faith deals with pain and suffering. They want to know why bad things happen to good people. They want to know where God is amid the tragedy and chaos on earth.

Being responsive isn't easy, but Jesus certainly showed us how to be responsive. He was patient and understanding with each question the apostles asked. He showed responsiveness every time Peter almost got it right. Jesus even had time for a woman who barely touched the hem of his garment. He loved the unlovable. He cared for the unpopular. Jesus even went to them instead of waiting on them to seek him out. So must we!

Adolescence is a tough time. Shifting social structures, shifting family structures, and changing bodies and minds characterize the teen years. One minute you are with the "in" group, and the next minute you're an outsider. One minute your parents are together, and the next minute they may be separating. One minute your body is that of a child, and the next minute you're dealing with adult features and adult feelings. One minute you're cute when you act out, and the next minute you're annoying. There are so many shifts and changes during the teenage years.

Some place has to provide a safe haven for processing these changes. Church should be that place! Amid shifting cultural norms, let the church represent "sanctuary" and "community" in the best sense of these words. Let us love one another with truth and grace.

Someone has to be a safe and trusted resource to help teens process these changes. Church leaders and teachers should be those resources! As they experience maturing bodies, confusing emotions, and shifting thoughts, let us be the "solid rock" of understanding and guidance.

This book is an attempt to help those who work with young people. Our intention is not to prescribe for you an out-of-the-box approach or present a one-size-fits-all Bible model. We will not even outline three points and a prayer to help you teach.

Instead, we present a "cafeteria" of ideas that apply to youth and can help you grow as a teacher, leader, worker, or parent of young people. Pick and choose what you need as if you were in line at a cafeteria. While we based this writing on the issues of a Sunday school class, you can use the ideas in any youth teaching/learning event. Take the ideas presented here and apply them to your teaching/learning/leading event. Our desire is for you to learn from what we have learned.

One purpose for writing results from our years of trying to encourage, affirm, train, and walk beside the many youth teachers and youth workers with whom we have worked. To all of you who have been co-laborers with us, God's best as you continue on this pathway.

Our other purpose for writing results from our years of working with teenagers. During those times of encouraging, affirming, training, and walking beside the many teens, they have taught us much about how to be better teachers. To all of you who have been co-learners with us, thank you for the grace you've given us when we've not been very good teachers.

Chapter One

The Wonderful World of Teens— Youth and Culture

We have a lot in common with teenagers, and yet we know so little about them. We have been the same age as those precious faces in our classes, yet we do not totally understand what is going on underneath their adolescent exteriors. We, too, have faced the joys of growing, learning, and friends and also the fears of acceptance, rejection, a wrong locker combination, acne, and dating. But today's teenagers seem to be different than many of us were at the same age. Aristotle wrote,

> [They] are passionate, irascible, and apt to be carried away by their impulses. They are slaves, too, of their passion . . . . If the young commit a fault, it is always on the side of excess and exaggeration for they carry everything too far, whether it be their love or hatred or anything else. They regard themselves as omniscient and are positive in their assertions; this is, in fact, the reason for their carrying everything too far.[1]

Aristotle's ancient description of the turbulent teenage years is as appropriate now as it was back then. Teenagers are the same today as they were yesterday. However, today's adolescents are different than the teens who have come before them. Our challenge as Sunday school teachers is to understand this new creation.

Understanding teenagers can be a frustrating exercise. We were once teens, so we should have some idea about who today's youth are.

Still, we only have a little idea. Some days we think we know exactly what is happening. On other days we are not even sure they are human.

Adolescence is that wonderfully turbulent time of life when a person grows both physically and mentally from a child into an adult. Throughout history, the ages and events that mark the beginning and ending of childhood have changed. Puberty begins earlier now than it did thirty years ago. The once-sacred age of eighteen no longer means that someone is an adult.[2]

Youth Sunday school teachers get to sit on the front row and watch this transformation take place right. The shy, uncoordinated boy in the fall finishes the school year as an athletic, confident young man. The little girl interested in Barbie dolls in September heads into the next summer with boys on her mind. Each teenager is different. God created each of us individually with a unique personality and special interests, likes, and dislikes. Every teenager goes through a series of developmental tasks as they grow through their adolescent years.

Understanding the developmental process of teenagers will help you prepare interesting and engaging lessons. Understanding adolescence will help strengthen teacher-student relationships. Understanding adolescence can be a lifetime exercise of books, surveys, and interviews. However, appreciating adolescence goes a long way in developing meaningful relationships with teenagers who need to be taught and cared for in Sunday school.

Early Adolescence

Twelve-, thirteen-, and fourteen-year-olds are generally considered to be in early adolescence. However, some eleven-year-olds are already experiencing adolescent changes. This is the typical middle school group. They are an active, loud, fun, and energetic bunch. They struggle with their sense of identity and place high importance on close friendships. These close friendships can influence everything from clothing styles to extracurricular activities. Parents get left out of the equation, and teenagers are occasionally rude to their parents.

Early adolescents realize for the first time that their parents are not perfect, and they tell them so. They begin the search for new people to love in addition to their parents.

Physically, they begin to grow and mature. Girls usually grow faster than boys at this age. It is not uncommon to find a room full of tall girls and short boys. With these "new bodies," they take on a greater ability to work and are able to express themselves with their actions instead of just their words. Early adolescents typically have mostly same-sex friends and participate in group activities. As their bodies begin to mature, there is some shyness, blushing, and modesty. Girls have their first period and begin to see their bodies develop curves. Many boys, however, do not begin any significant growth. As the boys do begin to grow, they develop a new sense of clumsiness, which can be a source of embarrassment in their social groups. Still, as soon as they gain coordination and realize they can show off, they do. With all of this growth and change going on, everyone worries about being "normal."

As they search for their identity in the world, middle schoolers begin to test the limits and find out exactly where the "line" is. Some of their acting-out behavior is harmless. They only want to see how far they can go and not get in trouble. With their dependence on friends and their reliance on the group, they occasionally experiment with tobacco, marijuana, and alcohol.

Middle schoolers are challenged in their classrooms at school to think and process information. Although they are still mainly concrete thinkers, they are capable of some abstract thought.[3]

Enter a Sunday school class full of early adolescents and you will probably see boys sitting on one side of the room and girls sitting on the other side. If possible, at least one chair will separate the two groups. The girls chat wildly with each other, and the boys sit or have quiet conversations. Younger boys usually "act out," according to most adults—drawing on the board, throwing paper or pens, being disruptive, etc. When the class begins, the talkers take over. These are the students a teacher loves. They answer questions, ask questions, and generally keep the class alive. The talkers can be girls or boys. Younger adolescents might not understand the concept of being quiet and will continue to disrupt the class. The hour spent teaching this group is full of frenetic energy.

Middle Adolescence

Middle adolescence usually occurs in ninth and tenth graders, late fourteen-year-olds to late sixteen-year-olds. This group generally struggles with unrealistically high expectations and a poor self-concept. They complain that their parents interfere with their independence. For most of this age group, body image and appearance are major concerns. In addition, there is also a mixed feeling of strangeness toward their bodies. The high regard they had for their friends a few years earlier begins to lower, and they withdraw from some of those friends. With this new awareness of their old friends, they begin to make new friends. They place a strong emphasis on the new peer group as it was selected with a sense of superiority and competitiveness. They also turn inward as they examine their life experiences. Journalizing or keeping silent about their daily activities is common.

With the focus on body image and appearance, this age is concerned about their sexual attractiveness. They frequently change relationships as they quickly experience feelings of love and passion. Their concerns about body image and their search for identity moves them toward heterosexuality, as they fear homosexuality. In their minds, they cannot be labeled "different."

For the first time in their lives, middle adolescents show evidence of thinking more deeply. This comes as a joy to their parents and teachers. The young people begin to form their own ideas and actually voice them to their friends—as long as they will not be labeled "different." They develop ideals and begin to select role models. They show consistency in moral code or conscience. They have a greater capacity for setting goals. They are interested in moral reasoning. Much of their world is black and white.[4]

Middle adolescents are concerned about what everyone thinks about them—especially the opposite sex. Individuals in peer groups tend to look the same. Anyone "not normal" is shamed and ridiculed. Friendships that were incredibly strong in middle school suddenly fall apart. Boys become important to girls and girls become important to boys. Driving a car and getting a driver's license are the main events in their lives.

Many of the walls formed in early adolescence are knocked down in middle adolescence. Boys might actually sit next to the girls in Sunday school. However, the group dictates the behavior of most of the individuals. Fitting in and being a part of the group are extremely important, and for one person to know all the answers is not a "cool" thing unless the group blesses the knowledge. If the peer leaders of the group participate or deem the activity or lesson to be "okay," then the rest of the group usually becomes involved. Social activities, especially those away from church, become the topics of conversation when the group gets together. Whining and complaining about parents is a regular part of these teens' vocabulary.

Late Adolescence

Late adolescence is typically seen in high school juniors and seniors. This group has a firmer understanding of their identity and can think through ideas. They have asked the question, "Who am I?" and they have an idea about the answer. They have a strong ability to express their ideas in words and other creative methods. They have a developed sense of humor. Their interests last more than one week at a time. Emotionally, they are stable and capable of making their own decisions. Compromise happens at this age. They take pride in their work as they rely more often on themselves. They exhibit a greater concern for others.

They are concerned with serious relationships as they have a clear sexual identity. They have the capacity for tender and sensual love. That tender and sensual love is expressed in sexual activity. Many late adolescents are sexually active as they seek ways to convey this love to their boyfriend or girlfriend. Though physically equipped for sexual activity, most of them may not be emotionally equipped and need our guidance!

This age group is capable of useful insight and has the ability to set goals and follow through to reach them. Personal dignity and self-esteem are important. These teens' accept social institutions and cultural traditions.[5]

High school juniors and seniors are almost adults. As "almost adults," they exhibit many of the same behaviors and patterns of adults. This age group thinks and talks and reacts much like their parents, schoolteachers, and other adults. Their ideas might seem childish because their life experience is still forming, but they are able to have adult conversations.

They commit to something for the long-term, whether it is sports, music, drama, volunteering, or relationships. Keeping commitments to their teams or clubs or groups is important because some of their identity is found in these groups. They want desperately to be free, yet deep down they yearn for boundaries in their lives. They understand the world, or at least their interpretation of the world, and can share their interpretation.

The Sunday school teacher for this group does not have to rely on activities and worksheets to pass the time and teach the lesson. Late adolescents generally want to talk about issues that are important to them. Many times, simply throwing a controversial passage of Scripture at their feet will result in a forty-five-minute discussion/debate about what is right and what is wrong and how God fits into everything. This conversation could not happen in the other stages of adolescence.

The developmental stages of adolescence help us understand today's teenagers. We can use the developmental stages as a background because we, as adults, have survived our teenage years. What separates this generation of teenagers from all other generations of teenagers is the culture in which they live. Many parents and teachers try to relate to their teenagers by saying they understand what it is like to be a teenager. Parents and teachers do understand what being a teenager is like, but they do not understand what being a teenager in the twenty-first century is like. The culture of today's teenagers is drastically different than what any adult experienced in high school.

Today's teenagers have been called the "Millennials," the "Mosaic Generation," and "Gen Z." Regardless of the label placed upon them, this group of teenagers will be the most numerous generation in American history. They are predicted to number more than 76 million and will live longer, be the best educated, have the most money, and be the most wired/wireless generation in history.[6]

As this group moves through the traditional stages of growth and development, they also exhibit behaviors not normally seen from such a young generation. The Barna Research Group, a company that specializes in research for Christian churches and church-related groups, has done extensive research on this new group of teenagers. When Barna compared this generation to previous teenage generations, they found that this group appears to be more upbeat, less cynical, less skeptical, and less pessimistic about life. Career development and maintaining a viable career are important. Education is preparation for life instead of a means for proving worth and acceptance from parents. Relationships are extremely important to this group, and they feel more connected to other people. Religion and spirituality are positive dimensions in life, but neither are central nor critical for their ultimate fulfillment.[7]

Cultural Influences

Each group of teenagers tends to be defined by the music and culture of their time. The "British Invasion" of the 1960s was replaced with the Disco of the 1970s, which gave way to Punk and New Wave music in the 1980s, which evolved to the Dance Club Pop Music of the 1990s. The black and white "Pong" video games of the mid-1970s have evolved into high-definition action-adventure games. Telephones with rotary dials have been replaced with cell phones that have Internet capabilities. Computers that once took up entire rooms are now light and portable. Times have changed, and those changes have affected teenagers.

MUSIC

Music might be the single most important cultural item for each generation. Each group can claim an artist, a group, or a style of music as their own. The words of the songs have something to say, both good and bad, about the times. Music reflects the tone of the world experience. It produces a life philosophy with which a generation can identify. Music provides heroes, helps define norms and values, and shapes the lifestyles of listeners.

The unique quality about this generation of teenagers is that no one single artist or style of music is the main influence. A quick glance through the music collection of a typical teenager will reveal an interest in pop, rock, rap, Christian, country, alternative rock, and maybe even jazz. Regardless of the style of music, the message is what binds all the genres with the teenagers. Music takes life situations and provides answers and responses for teenagers. Music takes life and makes sense out of it.

Years ago, music stores dominated the teen market. Teenagers bought records, cassette tapes, and CDs. Today, most teenagers get their music through the computer with file sharing, mp3s, and streaming audio. Music is immediately available. With the click of the computer's mouse and a CD burner, teenagers can "mix" a studio-quality compilation of their favorite music.

Music videos and the intense media coverage of the music industry dictate the latest in fashion and fads for teenagers. Hairstyles, shoes, and clothes are all products of the latest and greatest music act. What is interesting is that teenagers from all different races and cultures copy what they see and hear from all the different artists. It is not unusual for suburban, upper-class teens to dress and act like urban rap artists. Urban females might be enamored with the latest pop princess. Country is no longer relegated to Nashville and the South. Teens readily accept any music they feel identifies who they are and can help them with life's situations. They do not remain with those artists who necessarily look and act like they do.

You need to be aware of the current trends in music and fashion. The hottest artist one week might disappear the next week. Pay attention to who the teens emulate and the words the artists use. Every now and then, tune your radio to the popular teen station and listen to both the music and the words of the songs. Look through a few magazines like *Rolling Stone* or *Billboard.* Ask your teenagers what they are listening to. These simple exercises will provide a wonderful insight into their world. With that insight, we can begin to understand our teens a little better.

Some teens listen to specific artists simply for the shock value it produces from their parents. More than likely, we did the same thing. Do not judge the teens' musical choices and tell them those choices are bad. Accept the teenager for who he or she is and where he or she is. We do not have to listen to what they listen to, but we should love them regardless.

One word of caution about teenagers and their music: Do not try to turn back into a teenager in order to get them to like you. Do not show up for Sunday school dressed like a sixteen-year-old, talking like a seventeen-year-old, and singing songs popular with the fifteen-year-old crowd. Teenagers want and need their own language. Music is a huge part of that separate identity from adults. They need that separation as they begin to understand their identity. For us to totally embrace their culture and make it our own is destructive and inhibits them from growing. If some "teenage" music resonates with you, fine. Sing and enjoy it. But be real with your enjoyment of their music.

TELEVISION, MOVIES, AND COMPUTERS

Today's teenagers are heavily influenced by what they see on television, the Internet, video games, and movies. This generation is surrounded by more images than any other generation to date in history. With so much input coming from these outlets, it is easy to understand that teenagers are affected by what they see. If life imitates art, then teenagers imitate what they see.

Television is in 99 percent of all homes in North America.[8] Americans have the opportunity to choose from more than 200 channels of entertainment. Programming options range from shopping networks to hardcore pornography. A survey done by the Corporation for Public Broadcasting found that children ages six to seventeen watch an average of 2.5 hours of television on schooldays and 4.33 hours a day on the weekend.[9]

Our teenagers are tuning in. They are watching and learning and applying those lessons to life. We need to be aware of how much and which shows our teens are watching. We can offer guidance to help them navigate through the good and the not-so-good programming options. With some creativity, we can incorporate the most popular show at the moment into our Sunday school class and use a video example of how the gospel is lived out or how the characters failed to live the gospel. Television is a powerful tool, and we cannot ignore its influence on our teens.

When our teens are not watching television on the weekends, they are either at the movie theater or watching a movie they rented. Movies remain a popular date and group activity for teenagers. Teenagers say that going to the movies is the number one thing for them to do. It is more important than having a boyfriend or girlfriend, dating, sports, shopping, going to the beach, or sleeping late. Teens are enamored with the big screen.

They are learning about life from the movies they see. Many teenagers learn about relationships, violence, love, and even sex by watching actors in a movie. While many of the lessons they learn are positive, many can also be destructive. We need to know what our teens are watching. Even though a movie is rated PG-13, the "13" is there for a reason. The language might be a too harsh for some middle schoolers' ears. "R-rated" movies are restricted to ages seventeen and above because younger eyes should not see many of the themes and images in the movies.

While we can preview what our teens see in movies and on television, we are all still trying to learn how to best adapt to the computer. The computer is an extremely important tool for this generation. It can be a personal jukebox, scrapbook, telephone, movie theater, and lifeline to the outside world. Teens use Instant Messaging (IM) to talk to friends across town and computer friends across the world. They download music and pictures and share stories and poems. They visit chat rooms and find "soul mates." They play video games against the computer or against an opponent in a different time zone. They research their term papers, and they read the latest newspaper. The computer can do almost anything.

Our kids are spending time with the computer. This generation is computer savvy. When many adults have trouble loading software or their computers crash, they ask their sons or daughters to fix the problem. Some schoolteachers do not ask for help from the school's computer expert; they simply ask one of their students to fix the problem. You need to be aware of what is out there and where your teens are spending time on the Internet. The computer can be a valuable tool to help stay connected with your youth, and it can also be a destructive force with all the information and images only a click away.

FRIENDS AND FAMILY

Back in the 1960s, the family had the greatest influence in the life of a teen. Twenty years later, friends replaced family as the most influential influence, with the media appearing at number three.[10] The "family dinner" has all but disappeared. If a family is fortunate enough to have a sit-down meal together, it is usually hurried by schedules before dinner and homework or other activities after dinner. Saturday mornings have turned into a frantic drive across town to the next soccer game instead of simply relaxing at home. Even Wednesday nights and Sunday mornings are no longer sacred times in many communities as outside events are planned on top of church activities.

Also, divorce is now common in many families. Children are juggled between two parents, and the family structure is spread out over two households. The love for teenagers might be incredibly strong from each parent, but the traditional family system has been ripped in two. Teenagers are affected by divorce. Some of them understand the reasons, but some just know that mom and dad are not living together anymore.

Most teens turn to their friends for emotional and spiritual support. Their friends understand what is going on because their friends are experiencing the same things. They listen to the same music and watch the same movies and do the same things. Parents, on the other hand, are old-fashioned and out of touch. Regardless of the accuracy of the information they receive, teens turn to their friends for help with homework, relationships, and sex. With the popularity and availability of cell phones, a friend is literally only a phone call away. And if the phone goes unanswered, then something must be seriously wrong with the friend.

With all the outside influences of music, television, the computer, and friends, it is easy to see how family gets pushed outside the sphere of influence for teenagers. We need to know that today's teenagers are still the same teenagers we were, but they are dealing with a totally different environment in which to grow up. Take a look at two typical teenagers who probably sit in your Sunday school class:

Courtney is a normal sixteen-year-old girl in the eleventh grade at Central High School in Your Town, USA. Mark, her younger brother, is an eighth grader at Your Town Middle School. Courtney and Mark's parents both work, but their dad works late many evenings. They are an anomaly in their town because many of Courtney and Mark's friends have to split time between divorced parents.

A typical week for Courtney includes school every day from 8 A.M. until 3 P.M. Immediately after school, she has band practice for three hours on Monday, Tuesday, and Thursday. On Wednesdays, she gets a break from band and goes to church from 5:30-8:00 P.M. for Wednesday night supper and youth group. During the week she has at least two hours of homework a night because she is taking college preparatory classes. She does not have time for a boyfriend right now, but she still talks on the phone or Instant Messages (IMs) friends every night. Friday nights are football games, and the band plays at all the home games and a couple of the away games. On Saturdays, she is involved in marching band competitions both in Your Town and in different cities across the state. Sundays are church days. She goes to Sunday school and worship and then out to lunch with her family.

On Sunday afternoons, she does her homework from the weekend and sleeps.

Courtney knows her schedule is incredibly difficult, but she loves being in the band and she wants to go to college. Thus, she has made the decision to be as busy as she is. She knows that if she was not busy doing band, she would be playing a sport and then baby-sitting on the weekends.

Mark's week is a little different from Courtney's, but not much. He has the same school responsibilities as his older sister, but instead of playing in the band, he is on the soccer team. Every day after school for two hours, Mark is at practice or a game. After practice, he comes home to do about an hour of homework. He does most of his homework at school, so he has some free time to play video games. He is starting to show an interest in girls and has found that IM-ing them is a wonderful way to have a conversation without having to use his voice. He spends about an hour on the computer each night building his new relationships. Mark also goes to church on Wednesday nights and Sunday mornings. Since he is only in middle school, he has less homework than Courtney and can hang out with his friends more often. They go to a movie on Friday night and hang out on Saturday.

Courtney and Mark spend time with their mom and dad when they can. The majority of the time spent with their parents is in the car going to or from a rehearsal or practice. Many times in the car, Mark is listening to CDs with his headphones on and Courtney is talking to her friends on her cell phone. Therefore, conversation with Mom or Dad might not happen in the car. Their parents do the best they can to teach and guide them, but the kids' schedules are so busy it is hard to find time to do it.

Their friends, what they see and read and hear on the radio, television, movies, and the computer heavily influence teenagers. Parents try hard to be a loving presence, but teenagers naturally push their parents aside. You should be alarmed at what is available to our young people and where they are getting information. It definitely is a different world than when we grew up. But teenagers still crave a personal, loving, caring human being who is there in the good times and the bad times. You have that incredible opportunity! You have the chance to spend time each week with a wonderful group of talented young people. Sure, they have electronic gadgets and gizmos and regularly chat with "friends" in Indonesia, but they are your Sunday school class. Take time to know who they are. Share with them what it was like for you "back in the day." Celebrate the trials and triumphs of adolescence together!

Notes

[1] Kenda Creasy Dean et al., *Starting Right* (Grand Rapids MI: Zondervan Publishing House, 2001), 41.

[2] Ibid., 52

[3] "Normal Adolescent Development," *American Academy of Child & Adolescent Psychiatry*, no. 57, May 1997. <http://www.aacap.org/publications/factsfam/develop.htm.>.

[4] Ibid.

[5] Ibid.

[6] George Barna, *Real Teens, A Snapshot of Youth Culture* (Ventura CA: Regal Books, 2001), 15.

[7] Ibid., 23.

[8] Walt Mueller, *Understanding Today's Youth Culture* (Wheaton IL: Tyndale House Publishers Inc., 1999), 137.

[9] Ibid., 138.

[10] Ibid., 68.

Chapter Two

What Youth Sunday School Is Not—Common Myths about Youth Sunday School

One Sunday a little boy exited his Sunday school class for two-year-olds and displayed the amazing piece of artwork from which his pride truly hung. "Look what I made, Daddy! It's a giraffe." It clearly was a giraffe, a yellow body with brown spots, a long neck extending to the sky, and a short plume of a tail. Two clothespins had been attached for the legs, thus allowing the animal to stand on its own. On one side of the giraffe, the following words were written: "God made the wild animals (Genesis 1:24, 25)." The first thought of this boy's father, who also served as the church's youth minister, was of the Bible lesson that day. He thought about how special the story of creation is and the wonder it sparks in the imagination of a child. His second thought was as an educator. He considered those poor teachers as they tried to glue brown spots and yarn onto a piece of paper, surrounded by two-year-olds armed with scissors; still, what a great way to teach the story of creation! His third thought turned to the teachers he had left minutes before in the middle school classes. God did make the "wild animals," particularly the ones that surround the teachers every Sunday morning. They complain about the lack of breakfast. They separate into tribes of boys on one side of the room and girls on the other. They test the teachers who stand before them, eyeing them like hungry prey.

When you consider what forces are at work in the lives of teenagers, from social, to physical and emotional, and much less spiritual, it is amazing that they are able to pay attention to much of anything a teacher says at 9:45 on a Sunday morning. Yet week after week they return to occupy a seat. The first question to ask oneself is not "Why are they here?" Whether they are there by choice or if they have been dragged kicking and screaming, the fact is that they are there. The second question to ask is "Now that they are here, what do I do with them?" Before you explore too much regarding the structure and tools that will assist you in teaching the students in your class, consider the parameters listed below. They will help you understand Sunday school by recognizing what Sunday school is not.

The following fifteen statements are divided into three categories. The first is about the structure of Sunday school. These five misconceptions will draw attention to ideas about Sunday school that teachers need to know but often are not told prior to entering the classroom. The second is about you, the teacher. What is expected of you as you face students on a weekly basis and fill their minds with lessons from the Bible? It may be different than what you think! The final category is about the teaching time. When teachers enter the classroom, they come with preconceived ideas about how they should look, act, and teach as well as what they assume the students will be like and to what they will respond. You may find that you agree with some of the statements; you may find that you don't. The purpose for examining these ideas is to help you define your expectations of Sunday school. Many of the myths are based on common mistakes people and churches tend to make in their youth classes or departments. By making yourself aware of these misconceptions, you will be freed to try new things, increase enthusiasm, and have a more pointed direction as you make your youth Sunday school class the best that it can be.

Structure

Myth #1: Sunday school should be based on the public education model.

"Rich and poor alike depend on schools and hospitals which guide their lives, form their world view, and define for them what is legitimate and what is not. Both view learning on one's own as unreliable."[1] This statement is one person's view on how public education has hindered the learning process of society. The notion that becoming a system of rules and guidelines prepares students for end-of-grade testing and college entrance exams is corruption of the ideology of education.

The church plays a different role. The goal in Sunday school is not preparing for end-of-grade testing. The goal for the learners is to experience the love of Christ, developing a relationship with him. This relationship is personal and intimate. It comes from the heart of the believer, not a Sunday school book. All activities and lessons in a Sunday school class are tools God uses to teach humanity about Christ. Your example as teacher, the Scripture, and the relationships between students all play a role. You give students the tools to read the Bible for themselves and allow the Holy Spirit to help them interpret it for their lives. According to the quote above, "learning on one's own is unreliable." Thus, do not feel like your classroom must be managed like a schoolroom; instead, create an environment that encourages students to learn from each other, from the Scripture, and then continue learning on their own.

In public schools, classrooms are age graded and all the activities are developmentally appropriate. The culture of the Christian community is one of corporate worship, familial fellowship, and lifelong learning. Plan activities for your youth class that embrace these ideals. Have socials with senior adults. Teach children's classes. Engage dialogues between youth and their parents. Challenge yourself, your students, and your church to see beyond the compartmentalization of the ages.

Myth #2: Sunday school is just for small children.

Most everyone you ask to describe Sunday school automatically begins in the children's area. Do you ever wonder why we grab hold of this memory as the place to remember, usually fondly, Sunday school? It could be the felt boards and Bible pictures. It could be the apple juice and goldfish crackers. Life was easier and we were freer to explore and express our creativity. We cut, glued, and colored our way through the great stories of the Bible. We ate animal crackers when learning about Noah, wore colorful capes when hearing of Joseph, and made cotton-ball sheep when learning about the Shepherd. Then we became teenagers and all of that stopped. Suddenly we were no longer able to have snack in Sunday school. We read the letters of Paul and someone introduced the Minor Prophets.

No wonder we remember Sunday school most fondly as children. It was more fun and interesting. But learning should not have changed so abruptly. Sunday school is not just for children. Even adults can learn in Sunday school. The implication here is not for youth and adult Sunday school classes to begin felt board lessons; instead, the idea is that Sunday school holds something for everyone. If students are expected not to learn or enjoy Sunday school, chances are that they will not do either. Teenagers are caught between two worlds, child and adult. For many, this is the time when they begin to think about faith for themselves, asking questions and possibly rejecting some of the systems of Christianity they learned as children. Teachers should strive for real learning in Sunday school, allowing discussion and encouraging exploration. If little is expected or if the lessons are taught for children or adults, students will miss the value Sunday school holds for them. Furthermore, we will miss a golden opportunity to assist them in their search.

Myth #3: Sunday school is easy.

Walk through the frozen foods section of your grocery store and look at the meals marketed to you. "Ready in 5 Minutes." "A Complete Meal for Your Family in 30 Minutes." "No Mess, No Fuss." A popular soup company even has a recipe book out for two-step meals. In your home, you may have a self-propelled lawn mower, a self-cleaning oven, and a microwave. Today's market is driven by products that make tasks easier, thus saving you, the consumer, time. The same cannot be said for Sunday school. Sure, there are products that come with all the tools and step-by-step lessons. There are even lessons that teach themselves with the aide of a television and VCR/DVD player.

Despite these tools, Sunday school is not easy. A great deal is expected from teachers. First, you are asked to commit a lot of your time. You spend time in preparation for Sunday. You are asked to be at church every Sunday. You make phone calls to students, go on youth trips, and occasionally catch a middle school orchestra concert. Secondly, you are asked to commit yourself. You build relationships with students. You share their hurts and joys. You tell personal stories from when you were their age so they can understand that you have been there too. If teaching Sunday school to teenagers were easy, Sunday school directors and youth ministers would have an easy job every fall recruiting teachers. The more you invest in the students, the higher your risk of hurt, but also the greater the reward. You are special because of what you do for students.

Myth #4: Sunday school is about the curriculum.

Curriculum for Sunday school is a multi-billion-dollar industry. Money is spent on marketing, packaging, and developing literature that will grab your attention so that you will become a loyal customer. Curriculum is also developed so that you as a teacher will have the opportunity to connect your students with God. The flaw is that curriculum is written for the masses, not just for your church. Never forget that curriculum is a tool; it is not Sunday school. A lesson is a piece of the puzzle. "The sad fact is that youth ministry resources, curricula, and training are far more likely to teach us how to chase youth in order to 'catch' them for the church, than how to lead them home to God."[2] The risk of adopting a lesson or curriculum as the "be all, end all" is that students' needs may get left behind. If you are building relationships with your students through phone calls and contacts, you will quickly become aware of where your students are. Your task then becomes preparing a lesson that meets them there and leads them closer to God. No preprinted curriculum can do that.

By no means is our intention to demonize Sunday school curriculum. Our intent is for you as the teacher to recognize that curriculum is a resource for you in the job of connecting students to God. A successful lesson is not getting everything done in forty-five minutes. Instead, a successful lesson is one that brings students a step further in their faith journey. That might mean only one of your objectives gets accomplished or that the lesson cannot be wrapped up nice and neat at the end of the hour. God has changed hearts throughout history, yet sometimes we educators struggle to allow God to lead or change our lesson plans.

Myth #5: Sunday school needs no vision.

Corporations and businesses spend a great deal of time and money developing vision or mission statements. They develop teams to study the topic, pay consultants large sums of money for their opinions, and spend time instilling the statement in the hearts and heads of employees. The church already has a mission statement written by God. It is called the New Testament. But what about your youth Sunday school class or department? Have you ever adopted a mission statement for your group of teachers?

First, let us examine why there is a need for a mission statement for your teachers. Any person working in an organization needs a buy-in. Youth Sunday school is no different. Teachers need to understand the purpose of teaching rowdy middle school students every week. They also need to understand the direction you are trying to provide for your students. This provides parameters for them as they teach. If something does not fit the mission statement, they should avoid it. For instance, if your mission is to develop a Bible teaching ministry that challenges students to change the world based on the example of Christ, then you should not teach a lesson based on the views of the Republican Party (or Democratic Party, either).

Second, consider how to develop this mission for your class or department. Begin with prayer, asking God to direct your thoughts and plans in the direction that will best help your students and teachers become the people God wants them to be. Encourage a group to begin discussing the idea and solicit input from several sources. Include your senior pastor, the minister of education, the minister of youth, teachers, parents, and, most importantly, students. Have a small group process this information and develop a working statement. Refine it and present it to the classes for their approval. The hard part follows. Live it.

Sunday school needs a direction. With everyone on the same page and working together, time is better spent, frustration is lessened and everyone knows the ultimate purpose of your Sunday school.

Teaching Time

Myth #6: Sunday school is the primary Bible teaching hour of the week.

When you read this myth, your initial reaction may be, "If this is not the primary time, then what is?" Consider why it is not the primary teaching hour and you will probably begin to answer your own question. Examine the following checklist to see if these things influence your classroom during the Sunday school hour:

• Do your youth bring their Bibles?
• Do your youth study their lesson?
• Do you understand the motives behind the questions your students ask or the answers they give?
• Do you have the ability to gauge the absorption of the life lessons?

If you are like the majority of youth teachers, you do not get to see your students on a daily basis or discuss issues one-on-one. You interact with students on a limited basis and mostly in a church setting. You teach a prepared lesson that may or may not connect with their lives. Please understand that these facts do not reduce the importance of the Sunday school hour. Your influence during this time has the potential to change lives, but your time is limited. As a teacher, seek ways to encourage your students to study the Bible and learn through interaction with the text, friends, their family, and the spirit of God. At several places in this book, you will find ways to connect with your students and their families. Encourage them to develop a time of study on their own, searching for answers as well as better questions to ask.

Myth #7: Sunday school is just about teaching.

Who was the most influential teacher you ever had? Write down three lectures that person taught, and give as many details as you can remember. If you are like most people, you cannot remember many of the lectures you heard during your academic career. What, then, made your best teacher so influential? What about this teacher made you willing to listen to his or her opinion or advice? Why did you feel comfortable confiding in this person? The same answers you give are still true today. While teaching is important, never underestimate the power of relationships. You earn the right to be heard and to influence students, and the opportunity to show Christ's love depends largely on your ability to build relationships. The Sunday school hour is not the easiest, nor the best place to build these relationships. It is a good time to teach and lay the foundation for relationships, but the bulk of the building comes during the week or through other activities and interactions.

Myth #8: Sunday school is boring or predictable.

Many Sunday school teachers believe the best way to teach youth is through lecture. The reasons vary from the ease of preparation to the idea that it is easier to control teenagers when you lecture them. If you are like most learners, lecture does not exactly stimulate your creative thought. When we hear "lecture," we often equate it with disciplinary action from our mothers or huge halls filled with college students who are little more than a number. Neither of these are fond memories. Why, then, do we teach youth in such a manner as to conjure images of discipline, boredom, or school?

Sunday school should not be boring. For a few moments each week, we have the opportunity to place pearls of wisdom before youth who desperately need to learn about God, God's love, and the Christian faith. Yet we give them lecture. Worse yet, they know what is coming: roll call, prayer requests, lecture, and closing prayer. Sunday school should not be predictable.

Numerous publishing companies offer a wealth of teaching resources. Many, like the Smyth & Helwys youth curriculum *Intersection,* are filled with creative ideas, relevant topics, and stimulating questions. Browse the shelves at the local Christian bookstore, or search online at sites like NextSunday.com for ideas that will excite the learners in your class. As a teacher, be prepared to invest time into planning the lesson and preparing for extra ideas that remove the predictable. Brainstorm with other teachers or educators from the church and community to learn about what they are doing. Borrow their ideas and adapt them for your class. Most of all, have fun as you teach. The more excited you are about the lesson, the more excited your learners can become. By the way, when was the last time you were genuinely excited about teaching a lesson?

Myth #9: Sunday school is like "casting pearls before swine."

The previous myth talked about the pearls of wisdom you have the opportunity to share with your students. It is easy to consider your sixth grade boys as the swine. Admit it, they can drive you crazy! They create noises with their bodies, make faces at the girls, and throw paper at each other. The seniors might drive you nuts too. They come in and talk about the weekend, college applications, and the prom. They most certainly are not there to listen to you. If you have ever felt this way, it may have been justified; however, you have more influence than you realize.

The truth is that teaching students can be frustrating. Teaching can seem as fruitful as nailing Jello to a wall. Keep two things in mind when you get frustrated about no one paying attention: First, they are paying a lot more attention than you realize. Some hear your words and will adopt some of what you say as part of their lives. You are planting seeds and nurturing their growth. Others will never remember anything you say, but they will remember that you gave your time, you cared about them, and you set a Christian example. They will name you as someone who made a profound impact on their lives, despite not being able to recall the details of a single lesson ten years later. Think about it. How many Sunday school lessons do you remember from your days as a youth? How many teachers do you remember and the impact they had on you?

The second thing to remember is that you are not able to make a single person accept faith in Jesus or the truth of his teachings. That is God's role. Consider this old Hasidic saying: "It is not within our power to place the divine teachings directly in someone else's heart. All that we can do is place them on the surface of the heart so that when the heart breaks they will drop in."[3] You are an instrument of God, preparing students for an encounter with the Eternal. You communicate the love of God and the peace of Christ, but ultimately, only the student can choose the way of Christ.

Myth #10: Sunday school is for nerds.

Maybe the body language of a few students communicates that they are too cool to be here. Perhaps the bags under the eyes, from being at a party too late the night before, say the same thing. Whatever the reason, some students may feel that Sunday school is for nerds. In the hormone, popularity driven world of students who do not want to stand out for a stupid or non-cool action, answering questions about God, the Bible, and morality may make them feel uncomfortable.

The challenge is to create an atmosphere of learning that promotes student interaction on various levels. Breaking into small groups and writing a song about teenage angst has nothing to do with God, but it engages learners. Applying Paul's writings to Timothy in 1 Timothy 4:12 to the feelings of angst is turning the thoughts of a song into a lesson. Searching teen magazines for images that the media tries to sell teenagers is not necessarily about God, but it is engaging. Applying the words of the 139th Psalm makes self-image a lesson.

If you empower your students to be too cool for the lesson, then you have done them a disservice, but if you find ways to engage them, you might see that they can learn and listen despite the body language or eye bags. Making Sunday school interesting or cool is not about altering your image as a teacher; it is about making the truths of God applicable to the lives of teenagers.

Teachers

Myth #11: Sunday school ignores relationships.

When we go grocery shopping at our neighborhood chain, we are rewarded for being a repeat customer. By scanning the handy card attached to our key rings, we receive product discounts and coupons that can be accumulated and redeemed for special prizes. Buying groceries has never been better. Oddly enough, when we receive mail from this same grocery store, the coupons or specials advertised are often products we purchase regularly. This could be chalked up to coincidence, but the truth is that the handy key ring card is not only giving us discounts, but rather recording every product we buy and placing it in a huge database that identifies the needs of our family and how the grocer can meet those needs.

In an odd sort of way, we have quite a relationship with that grocery store. We also realize that the church can learn a lot about relationships from this model. If a grocery store thinks it is important enough to save information about us through our purchases in order to send coupons that will bring us back, then teachers who work with students ought to realize the premium of relationships as well. Great teachers build relationships with students through interpersonal contact outside the classroom. Relationships bring people back to Sunday school. Everyone wants to feel as if they are cared for. You have the ability to provide this. So for every minute you spend preparing a lesson, spend two making contacts with your students. Relationships earn you the trust to be confided in and the right to be heard.

Myth #12: Sunday school will be okay with "warm bodies."

Have you ever entered a fast food restaurant and been greeted by an unsmiling, unfriendly, and generally disagreeable person behind the register? After they make you feel welcome, they proceed to mess up your order regardless of how slowly and clearly you speak. Then despite your best efforts to be friendly, they look at you like you kicked their puppy. Do you ever wonder how a person like this is able to keep a job? It is amazing how some people get hired, as if the manager simply needs a "warm body" to work.

Warm bodies are not good answers to problems of staffing. Often they make the issue worse. Knowing this, we sometimes have to recruit volunteers through guilt or blackmail to bring them into youth Sunday school. The students have a teacher then, at least technically, but how successful will that unwilling volunteer be to do outreach, build relationships, and teach creatively? Youth Sunday school will survive these periods, but unless the person turns from a caterpillar into a butterfly, it probably will not thrive.

Develop volunteers over a period of time. You may need to develop a mentoring program for new teachers or provide workshops to help them with new ideas and "how-tos." Free them up the first year to be a teacher who builds relationships while another person teaches. Do this to avoid frustration and burnout, thus avoiding high turnover and inconsistency. Warm bodies are great, but a heart for teaching is contagious!.

Myth #13: Sunday school is about you.

If you have ever had a teacher or professor in school who had a huge ego, you understand the need to address this myth. Not only were such teachers unwilling to entertain questions or debate, but they were usually not approachable. We have known teachers in high school who demean someone for asking the teacher to clarify a point. Can you imagine that person teaching Sunday school? Not a pretty picture! Sunday school is about the students and their faith journey. You are there as a guide along the way. Students should be encouraged to ask questions, to disagree with you and one another, and to be wrong.

Many teachers have said they learned more as a teacher than they ever did as a student. Use the information you learn to enhance the lesson for the students. Be wise enough to recognize when some material would be inappropriate for your students or irrelevant to the lesson. They think you are smart anyway, so do not worry about impressing them. Worry about engaging them.

By maintaining the focus on connecting the students with God, you will be able to learn and grow personally as well as grow a heart for the students with whom you teach. Allow yourself to look silly, have fun with students, and learn from and with them.

Myth #14: Sunday school is "solitary" for teachers.

Once you are asked to teach, you may think you are left on a deserted island with absolutely no help. If that were the case, we would not blame you for a short tenure. There are so many helps for you as the teacher that a book could probably be written just on resources and contacts. For our purposes, we will look at a few areas where teachers can gain support and community.

The first place to gain support is through other adult relationships. You may have a co-teacher who shares responsibilities or teaches in other Sunday school classes. Another way to gain support is by building relationships with the parents of the students. Another way is to look among other adult relationships is your "home" Sunday school class. Petition members to help you teach once in awhile. Seek prayer support from them and attend class functions with them outside the Sunday school hour. You need to maintain your mental health through good adult relationships.

A second place to find assistance is in the ministry staff of your church. This list may include a Sunday school director as well as staff ministers. Let them know your needs and they can assist you or direct you to the third area of support, training and curriculum. Remember that these are tools to help you connect with your students. Research them and learn at your own pace. Few people have ever complained about receiving too much technical training. If for any reason you ever feel isolated, make sure you voice that to someone who can help you. The church is a community and you should never feel left alone.

Myth #15: Sunday school is planned in the car (or on Saturday night).

Brian Foreman writes, "when I was in college, I worked at a church for the first time. The children's minister was also a college student. We became good friends and carpooled to church on Sundays and Wednesday nights. I can remember several Sunday afternoons when, as we drove to the church to conduct our programs, she asked for ideas for her program that night."

Our hope is that this story makes you a little angry about irresponsibility. Unfortunately, many Sunday school teachers from cradle to grave classes plan the same way. They read their lesson on Saturday night, sketch a quick outline, and then fall asleep. Sunday morning goes fine and they assume that what they are doing is fine. Imagine the potential for a great Sunday school that is left unlocked when a teacher gets by with a hastily prepared lesson. Aeneas Williams, a cornerback in the NFL, describes why after numerous Pro Bowls and over eleven seasons in the league, he is still the first player on the field at practice and the last to leave. His explanation is that he wants to live his life and do his job to the fullness of his potential. What a powerful example to set for young players in the league!

To begin unlocking your additional potential, try this method of planning: Read the lesson in the student book and corresponding Scripture on Sunday evening. Read the Scripture and lesson foci again on Monday, Tuesday, and Wednesday. Live with the lesson throughout the course of the week. On Thursday, read the lesson from the teacher book and jot preliminary ideas for the lesson along with observations you have had during the week. Read only the Scripture on Friday. On Saturday morning, put together the final lesson plan. Ideally, this will only take two to three hours of your time during the week, but on Sunday morning you will be prepared to apply the lesson through telling current events, sharing personal stories, and making the lesson real to the students. Challenge the students to prepare for the following Sunday in a similar manner. Just remember to live each day striving to fulfill the potential God has placed inside of you.

Notes

[1] Ivan Illich, *Deschooling Society* (New York: Harper & Row Publishers, 1970), 3.

[2] Kendra Creasy Dean and Ron Foster, *The Godbearing Life* (Nashville: Upper Room Books, 1998), 58.

[3] Mark Devries, *Family-Based Youth Ministry* (Downers Grove IL: InterVarsity Press, 1994), 160.

Chapter Three

Method in the Madness— Organizing for Growth

Have you ever noticed how much teenagers grow? You can literally watch seventh graders transform into high school seniors as they eat pizza after pizza. Physically, their bodies get bigger and taller. Emotionally, they become a little more secure and confident. Spiritually, we hope they have a better understanding about God and love and grace. Growth all happens right before our eyes, and sometimes we never see it happening.

Just as a teenager grows, we should also want our youth Sunday school to grow. In fact, the main goal for Sunday school should be growth. This growth takes shape in both biblical knowledge and in the number of the participants that meet each week to study the Bible. You have been given the charge to teach youth the Bible and have been encouraged to share the biblical story with as many people as possible. The Sunday morning time of study is the specific, traditional time set aside for people to learn about the Bible and the biblical story. It is a place where everyone can interact with others and learn about how God is working in their lives. Sunday school should be a time when teens can be real with each other and have the blessing to ask questions and search as we all struggle together on the journey of faith. The journey is easier when we are equipped with biblical knowledge and when fellow travelers of faith join us.

Growth during youth Sunday school occurs because you care and pay attention to your youth and provide a safe and inviting atmosphere for your class. When you focus on preparing for and caring for youth, you will notice your teenagers are more excited about being at church on Sunday morning. When your teenagers are excited about being at church on Sunday morning, they bring their Bibles and their friends!

Attention to these two areas should be a natural responsibility for you. Many of these ideas have been used since the beginning of youth Sunday school. A few of these suggestions might be more expensive than your church budget will allow. Some of them might be cutting-edge to you and seem to be more cultural than biblical. You know your youth better than anyone else. Sift through and pick nuggets that you think will work for your situation. Enlist the assistance of your youth to help you decide what might work and what will definitely not work. They will quickly tell you how they feel about different ideas. Remember, the goal is to grow spiritually as well as numerically.

It All Starts at the Top

Every organization needs a leader. People need to know who makes the final decision and who gives guidance and help. Sunday school is no different. If your youth Sunday school department is one class of teenagers or multiple classes of teenagers, designating a youth Sunday school division director is imperative. The youth Sunday school division director should not be the youth minister. Ideally, the director will be a caring adult who has a heart for youth learning the Bible. The main role of the youth Sunday school director is to oversee the youth Sunday school ministry.

The following is an example of a "job description" for a youth Sunday school division director. Use this as a guide and change what needs to be changed within your church situation and your Sunday school organization. Every church does not have a Sunday school council or a minister of youth or education. You know your system and structure. Make it work for you!

YOUTH SUNDAY SCHOOL DIVISION DIRECTOR

The youth Sunday school division director is responsible to the Sunday school director / minister of youth / minister of education for coordinating the work of the high school and middle school Sunday school division. The division director is directly responsible for modeling Christian growth through a commitment to the Bible teaching ministry of the church.

- Assist the youth minister, Sunday school director, and Sunday school council in discovering and enlisting new teachers, substitutes, and workers.
- Assist existing teachers in arranging for substitute teachers, classroom supplies, and teaching needs. Be aware of each class and its specific functions and personality.
- Coordinate classes and volunteers in the visitation/inreach ministry to members and prospects.
- Assist the youth minister, Sunday school director, and Sunday school council in communicating information concerning the total work of the Bible teaching ministry.
- Assist the youth minister, Sunday school director, and Sunday school council in involving all teachers and workers in training opportunities.
- Assist the youth minister, Sunday school director, and Sunday school council in discovering curriculum needs and leadership support materials for their specific age group division.
- Assist the youth minister, Sunday school director, and Sunday school council in providing ministry and support to the teachers of their specific age group division.
- Attend quarterly Sunday school council meetings.

Creating a job description will help the volunteer understand his or her role in youth Sunday school. The job description also sets boundaries between the leader and the teachers. Simple guidelines make the position easier to understand and less threatening.

The major responsibility of the director is to make sure the Sunday school teachers are prepared for the youth. One way to assist in teacher preparation is with a regularly scheduled teacher meeting. Some Sunday school groups choose to meet weekly, which might be too many meetings for some teachers' schedules. Other Sunday school groups meet once a year—which is not enough meetings. Find a time and a schedule that works best for you and your fellow teachers. During your teachers' meetings, make sure to include prayer, teacher responsibilities, and a brainstorming session. Other issues such as discipline, calendar events, and the sharing of stories will naturally become a part of the meetings.

Begin your meeting time in prayer. Set aside time to spend with God, signifying that this moment in your schedule is different. This time is to be spent preparing for the call you have answered to teach the Bible to teenagers. Pray for your teenagers as you seek to reach them with God's word. Pray for your fellow teachers as you all journey together. Pray for your church as you seek her support for the youth. Pray for yourself as you answer God's call to teach the Bible.

Determining who is teaching might seem like the simplest of tasks for teachers, but unfortunately, it can be the most frustrating aspect of Sunday school. This part of the agenda makes two assumptions: First, the youth Sunday school uses some type of Sunday school literature. Second, more than one person teaches in the department or individual class.

Look at each person's schedule at least a month in advance. Who is going to be out of town? Who will be available to teach? Are there any Sundays when a substitute teacher will be needed? Is the youth ministry planning any trips that will significantly deplete the Sunday morning numbers so that classes (or the entire department) need to be combined? By answering these questions in advance, everyone will know who is supposed to be where and when.

Many Sunday school classes have more than one teacher. This allows for more people to be involved in youth Sunday school without requiring them to be present for all fifty-two Sundays of the year. This practice also allows the team to work as a "lead teacher" and "assisting teachers" each Sunday. The lead teacher is in charge of the lesson. This person asks the assisting teacher to assist the lead teacher with whatever he or she needs: small group conversations, crafts, activities, etc. Inevitably, on some Sundays none of the regular teachers will be present for class. Vacations, work, time away, etc., take each of us away from church every now and then. Communicating schedules to other teachers reduces the likelihood of the youth waiting for a teacher who is not present.

Also, make sure everyone knows the lesson for those Sundays. The director should read the lesson every week, even if he or she is not teaching a class. Assuming Sunday school literature is used, the entire department will know which Sunday in November each class will be discussing Psalm 23, for example. If, however, a class is doing an individual book study or a study separate from the literature, communicate that information with the other teachers in the department. Sharing that simple piece of information might bring in a flood of ideas from other teachers or suggestions on how to use the study differently to effectively teach the youth. Brainstorm together. Other teachers have wonderful ideas about how to use a passage or incorporate an activity. Trust each other.

We have heard horror stories from Sunday school teachers who did not communicate well with each other. The class was supposed to use the literature provided for Sunday school by the youth ministry. One teacher followed the outlines and the teaching plans provided in the book. One teacher did not use the literature at all. This teacher decided to use whatever was "inspiring" that week. Both teachers talked to each other to make sure one of the two of them would be present for class, but that is as far as their conversations went. Their class could tell these teachers did not communicate well with each other. The lessons did not "flow" from week to week. Some Sundays, one teacher would come prepared to teach the lesson from the literature only to find out the other teacher planned to teach a lesson on teenage drinking and driving. These teachers did not have a regular meeting time, and the youth suffered.

Sunday school teachers do have a life outside of the church. Many are involved with numerous meetings at the workplace or with other organizations. Regardless of the situation, communication from the director to the Sunday school teachers can and needs to happen.

The Internet has opened up a world of communication. Email is becoming the most popular form of sharing information. It is fast, it can send a lot of information, and if people read their emails, it is an extremely effective way of keeping in touch with each other in this busy world.

In the time it takes to write a one-page letter, the director can share information about prayer requests, ideas about the coming week's lesson, dates of concern or conflict for the teaching schedule, include a list of prospects, etc. A weekly email is a wonderful way to stay connected with each other during the week. However, guard against the Internet as a way to totally replace teacher meetings; gathering together is important. Still, a weekly email can enhance any youth Sunday school.

In the Trenches

You are a wonderful creation of God! In my opinion, anyone who teaches youth Sunday school has a special place in heaven. Those who teach middle school will sit at the right hand of God! Caring adults who teach youth Sunday school do so because they love teenagers. They celebrate when their teenagers succeed and give support when their teenagers fail. They also want their teenagers to learn what is in the Bible and why those lessons and stories are important.

Contrary to popular belief, especially by teenagers, Sunday school does not "just happen." While it is true that Sunday arrives at the same time week after week, growing in Sunday school requires preparation and hard work. A strong leader will grow a biblically literate class and a room of youth who want to be at church on Sunday morning. Growth happens because the youth are prepared for and cared for.

Teenagers are smart. They know when you are prepared. They know when you have talked with other teachers about different teaching assignments. Teenagers know when you have prepared the lesson plan on the way to church and try to fool them into thinking you are ready for them. If you try to fool them too many times, they will stop coming. Teenagers do not want their time to be wasted. Their schedules will not allow for wasted time.

The chapter "Studying the Lesson—Preparing and Caring" covers the big picture of planning and preparing the lesson, which is vital to growth in Sunday school. But youth also pick up on the smaller items of preparation. Use this checklist to see how well you prepare for Sunday school.

- Do I pray for my class?
- Do I arrive at church and get to my classroom before my class?
- Do I have all the materials I need before I get to my class?
- Do I have all copies made before I get to my class?
- Once I get to my class, do I make sure the chairs and tables are ready?
- Once I get to my class, do I prepare the room for the first part of the lesson?
- When I see my class or other youth in the hallway, do I share a kind word or a smile?
- Do I feel ready for class to start when it is time for class to start?
- Am I "in charge" of class once we begin, or do I give control to the youth?

Many of these items change week to week, depending on the lesson and the materials required for each lesson. The teacher who opens the lesson book before Saturday night knows which materials are necessary and how many copies to make. Take a couple of weeks and critique yourself with this simple checklist. Then make the necessary changes to be better prepared.

Out in the World

Sunday school teachers also care for their teenagers. We have the wonderful opportunity to share an incredible journey with them because we see them every week. In this day of the busy teenager, you might actually spend more quality time with teenagers than their parents! We teach our youth that we care for them with our presence, with our words, and with our surroundings. When they see that we really do care about them, they will show much more interest in the things we say and the lessons we teach. When they show more interest, they pay attention and biblical growth occurs. They also tell their friends about "my wonderful Sunday school teacher," and more new faces begin showing up on Sunday mornings.

Make it a priority each semester to spend time with each person in your class outside of the Sunday school hour. Go see them play basketball. Listen to their chorus concert. Treat a small group to a banana split. When they invite you to see them in their school play, make every effort to attend. Granted, you cannot be present at every activity your teens do, but when you show up for at least one game or concert, you teach them that you do care about them. When you go up to them after the event to congratulate them, their friends notice "that strange adult." As soon as your teenager explains who you are, they wish they had "a strange adult" to come support them, too.

The words you use with teenagers are important. When you see your teenagers in the halls of the church, speak to them. If you see them at the mall or the movie theater, take stock of the situation and if the timing is appropriate, go over and say something. Yes, the teenager will probably be a little embarrassed, but deep down, he or she will be thrilled to know that you came over and spoke.

With all the different ways we can be connected today, we do a poor job of connecting. Cell phones, the Internet, email, and instant messaging are types of technology your teenagers use on a regular basis. Spend time learning how to use these incredible tools. If you have a cell phone, enter your student's cell phone numbers into your phone. Most phones have the capacity to hold more than 100 numbers. Use the numbers on a regular basis. Call after school, on the weekend, or whenever you might be thinking about one of your youth. A simple "I was just thinking about you and wanted to call" takes about thirty seconds. But the rewards from that phone call last much longer.

Also, use the Internet to communicate with your class. Email them a quick note. Send them an e-card. Create a weekly Sunday school newsletter and email it to the class in the middle of the week. Many Internet service providers have the instant messaging software as a part of the package. Figure out how to use instant messenger and "IM" your youth when you are online at the same time. It is amazing how many youth "talk" to each other online through "IM." If you do not know how to set up or use "IM," ask your class, we are sure one or more know how to do it.

If all of the new technology intimidates you or if you do not have access to a computer or the Internet, pick up the phone on a Tuesday night and say, "I was just thinking about you and wanted to see how your day went." Or find stationery or a postcard and actually write a quick note and mail it. Writing a note to a youth does require a little more work than email, but actually holding a handwritten card or letter makes us all feel loved and cared for. We all like to get personal mail.

A subtle way in which we care for our youth is through the space we provide for them. Unfortunately, many youth ministries are located in the basements or the attics of churches. These spaces "will be perfect for the youth. They will love it there." But adults would complain and go directly to the pastor if their Sunday school classes met in those same rooms. Some churches do have youth in "creative" spaces, and it works wonderfully. Some churches have built youth-only areas with classrooms, game rooms, coffeehouses, and auditoriums.

Regardless of where youth Sunday school meets in the church, the space must be warm, inviting, and appealing to teenagers. Freshly painted walls, clean carpet or tile, chairs with all four legs, and tables without carved initials on the tabletop are simple, yet important to an inviting room. After those basic needs are met, the rest of the decorating is up to you and your youth.

We have been in beautiful, brand-new education buildings for youth Sunday school that have immaculate hallways, beautiful paint, and comfortable furniture. Still, other than the blinds on the windows and a dry-erase board, nothing is on the wall. The building committee does not allow anything to be taped or tacked onto the walls. That is unfortunate. We have never been in a teenager's bedroom where the walls were bare except for a new coat of paint. Teenagers put up posters, quotes, pictures, and anything else they can attach to their walls. It gives them a sense of comfort and identity. The Sunday school room can provide that, too.

We are not suggesting that you go to the nearest music store and buy the latest band's poster and cover your Sunday school walls in swimsuit models. Still, put something interesting on your walls. Get school pennants or signs from the local high schools. Find posters that interest the entire class. Find the photographer in your class and have him or her take individual pictures of each student and make a collage. Ask your teenagers what they would like to see on their walls each Sunday. Be creative with the walls, but do not go overboard.

Get a bulletin board for "class community" announcements. Your teenagers can put up flyers or promotional literature about events they are involved in at school or in the community. Soccer schedules, football schedules, etc. can be posted for all to see and be invited. A summary sign of last week's lesson could be posed to remind the class what happened last week. The youth could be in charge of the bulletin board and its upkeep.

Provide appropriate music as students come into class each Sunday. Get a small CD player and a few popular Christian CDs. A couple of minutes before class begins, start the CD as background music. After a few weeks, your students will probably ask if they can bring some of their music to play.

The furniture in youth Sunday school is also important. Most classes use the same tables and chairs as the adults. Some classes use donated chairs, sofas, and beanbag chairs. Use furniture that is comfortable without being distracting. Sofas are wonderful pieces of furniture for "hanging out" and for fellowship but are not ideal for a learning environment. Beanbag chairs are incredibly comfortable but might not be best for Sunday school. Metal folding chairs are abundant but are cold and uncomfortable. Take stock of what is available and make wise decisions. We want the youth to feel comfortable and welcome. The furniture we use sends that message.

Finally, when it comes to creating a youth Sunday school classroom, ask the youth for their input. They are the target audience. They know what they like and dislike. Encourage their suggestions and creativity. However, keep in mind that you have the final say in what goes and what stays. Some of their ideas are wonderfully creative but totally impractical. Some of their ideas will not work in a church. Explain to them why. Use the creation process as a teaching moment. They will know that you care about them.

Sunday School in the Real World

The youth ministry of Your Town Church has three youth Sunday school classes. Celeste teaches the middle schoolers, Tim teaches the eleventh and twelfth graders, and Kathy teaches the ninth and tenth graders. Jeff, the youth Sunday school division director, gathers the youth into the assembly area at 9:45 A.M. each Sunday morning. After a few announcements and a prayer, he sends them off to their classes.

Celeste waits at the door for her group. They come trudging down the hall and take their time getting into the room. Finally, at 10:00, they are all inside. A little after 10:05, a late student, Ashley, comes in the door. Celeste, who had already begun the lesson on Psalm 23 by reading word-for-word out of the teacher's guide, has to stop the lesson. "It's good of you to finally join us this morning, Ashley. Have a seat. You interrupted me." Celeste goes back to reading the book word-for-word. The only time she pauses is when she asks a question from the book. When the class gives her the wrong answer or no answer at all, she sighs heavily and gives them the right answer.

By the end of class, the students are bored to tears, but Celeste feels good about giving them the lesson.

Next door, Tim waits for his class. He has the latest Steven Curtis Chapman CD playing and is excited to see the students enter his classroom. They run to get the beanbag chairs and a seat on the sofa. The first song finishes and Tim lets the next song begin. The students keep talking to each other about their weekends and plans for the next week. After the second song finishes, Tim begins class.

He tells the class that the day's lesson is on Psalm 23. Before they begin, he wants to do some "catching up." He asks each youth how their week was and what special or exciting things happened to them during the past week. Every youth is encouraged to share something. After fifteen to twenty minutes of "catching up," Tim asks for prayer requests. The youth, who were already looking at their watches, figure out that if they say enough prayer requests, the lesson will be shot. So they request prayer for everything they can think of and some things they make up. Some of the prayer requests are serious and heartfelt. But inevitably, the list grows to include "a friend at school has a brother in Tennessee who has a friend whose dog got hit by a car . . . ."

By the time the prayer is finally said, another twenty minutes have gone by. Tim, realizing it is already 10:40, says, "Well, it seems that time has slipped by this week. Instead of having our normal lesson, let's all listen to this new song on the CD." Tim plays a song and then dismisses the class for worship. He feels confident that the kids had a good time in his class.

Across the hall, Kathy waits for her class. Like Tim, she has music playing and is excited to see the teenagers come to her class. After everyone is in the room, she fades out the music and starts class. One of her seniors is late, but Kathy smiles when he comes in and continues with the lesson. She follows the activities prescribed by the teacher's guide, but has reworked one activity because she knows what works best for her class. She presents the lesson, encourages conversation, and makes sure the class understands the main point of the lesson. At 10:30, the lesson is over, but class is not. She asks the group how their week has been and if anyone has news or celebrations to share. The kids know this is not a "must-share" activity. After a few responses, Kathy turns the conversation toward prayer requests. The kids look at their watches and see it's 10:40. The prayer request list is concise but appropriate. After a time of group prayer, Kathy dismisses class at 10:50, leaving enough time for everyone to get to worship.

All of these classes are real. The names have been changed, but the approaches these teachers took have not. Teenagers complained about the first two teachers.

Celeste "is mean." "I hate being late for class; she gives me that look, like I've done something wrong." "We don't get a chance to say anything." "If we don't give her the answer she wants, she tells us we are wrong." "I don't like coming to her class." "I definitely don't want to bring a friend in there."

Tim "does not teach us anything." "We just show up and start talking and he never bothers to teach us the lesson." "It was fun the first couple of times, but I hate telling the class about my date on Friday night or the trip I took with the drama club." "Some of those prayer requests were the stupidest things I have ever heard. I know they made them up just so we wouldn't have to have a lesson." "I love sitting on the beanbag chair." "Bringing a friend to that class would be a waste of time."

"I love Kathy's class." "You can tell she wants to be there." "She is always prepared and teaches us about the Bible." "I love the way she encourages conversation and allows us to think, even if our answers aren't what the book's answers are." "I feel good about bringing friends with me to Sunday school."

Celeste was prepared for her students, but she never cared for them. She thought they were getting the Bible lesson, but she lost them as soon as they walked into her room. Tim cared for his students, but he never prepared for them. He felt great that they were comfortable and would share their lives in his class, but the Bible was rarely opened. Kathy prepared and cared for her class. She understood how important it was to have the lesson ready and to make the youth feel comfortable. Her balance led to growth in both biblical knowledge and in the number of students she had throughout the year.

Growth in youth Sunday school can happen when we pay attention to preparation and to our attitudes toward the youth. Place yourself in the shoes of a teenager. Would you want to go someplace where no one knew your name? Would you want to get up on a Sunday morning expecting to learn something about the Bible and get an hour of weekly stories? Would you want to have an adult friend show up at your chorus concert? Would you want to go see a couple of adults look totally clueless as they struggled to read the week's lesson from the book? Would you want to spend time with a group of adults who remembered your birthday and sent you a card? Would you want to spend time with a teacher who really listens to your problems and does not try to lecture you? You would go where you are prepared for and cared for.

If we are honest with ourselves, teens want the same thing. Let's give it to them. Prepare yourself, the lesson, the room, the department. Care for teenagers in class and in their world. If you can genuinely prepare and care for your class, your teens will be interested and excited about what is happening on Sunday mornings. They will want to learn more about what the Bible has to say for their lives. They will want to share that excitement with their friends. Your class will grow both spiritually and numerically.

Chapter Four

Studying the Lesson— Preparing and Caring

For years, our vision of ministry has been, "People go where they know they are prepared for and are cared for." This statement continues to be a guide and motivator for every aspect of our ministries. Still, nowhere is this vision more appropriate than when teaching youth.

When we guide and not manipulate the class session, when we are open to youth joining in interactive learning, we communicate preparation. When we have support materials ready, handouts prepared, and the room arranged, we communicate preparation. When we know exactly what the goals of our class session are, we communicate preparation. As we communicate good preparation, we also communicate that we care.

We are in the people business. If youth don't think we care about them, they will not participate! Effective preparation is one way to communicate that we care. As we contact them when they're absent and challenge them when they're present, we communicate that we care. As we cry with them when they hurt and celebrate with them in their joy, we communicate that we care. People go where they know they have been prepared for and are cared for!

"Prepared for and cared for" doesn't happen automatically. We have to be intentional. Being intentional means we schedule and protect times for study, for daily preparation, for prayer and practice. Effective teachers prepare so that they can help others learn, grow spiritually, and grow communally.

As we prepare and teach intentionally, we can anticipate several outcomes:

(1) *Growth in belief*—As God's Word challenges us, we grow deeper in our spirituality. Consistently encountering biblical truth leads to closeness with God and with one another. As we grow in our beliefs, we are better prepared to be servants in the kingdom of God. Intentional teaching helps us lead youth to deeper spiritual maturity.

(2) *Growth in belonging*—As God's Word challenges us, we grow deeper in our intimacy with one another. There is no way to sit in a Sunday school class week after week and not grow friendships! Growing friendships in our class then helps us reach out to others, both inside the church and outside the church. Intentional teaching fosters relationships that add meaning to the body life of the church family.

(3) *Growth in becoming a servant*—As God's Word challenges us, we grow deeper in our service to one another. We don't teach to entertain; we teach to equip. As we teach with purpose and intentionality, we challenge those youth in our classes to grow in their own service. We are all called to be servants of Christ. As we grow in our servanthood, we enrich the church.

(4) *Growth in being present*—If we are growing in belief, community, and servanthood, the message of our "great" class is going to spread. Most youth want to be around good things that are happening. Your youth will tell others in the church about the class. Your youth will tell others not in the church about the class. You will begin reaching out more; you will begin reaching in more. Intentional preparation leads to effective teaching. Effective teaching leads to growth!

Six Tips for Preparation

The following tips will help you begin to be more intentional about communicating "prepared for and cared for" to those who come to your class.

(1) *Acceptance* —Accept the Learner where he/she is. You will have some youth learners who have been in church all their lives. You will have others who have just begun to attend. Your preparation will help you be ready for all learners, regardless of their level of knowledge and Christian maturity. You must be flexible, and nothing helps you be more flexible than preparation. God is guiding the process! Your task is to love and care for each young person who comes into your classroom. Your task is to guide them as they search for meaning from Scripture. They will grow in God's love. Teach them, love them, and help them grow. Leave the results to God!

(2) *Growth and development*—Be aware of the developmental stages of your youth. They are maturing in many different stages. Some middle schoolers may more closely resemble older youth while some may more closely resemble older children. Pay attention to these stages and be flexible as learners grow and develop. Prepare for a wide spectrum of learners and maturity levels.

Know your youth learners personally, accept them as individuals, and be flexible. Preparation will let you anticipate your various learners and let you have several learning approaches ready to respond to their needs.

(3) *Motivation*—Try to understand the "why" and "what" of youth learners. "Why" do they attend Sunday school? "What" do they really want to learn? Pay attention to the friendships they have and make, pay attention to their parents' expectations, and be sensitive to the needs of each person in the class. As you understand better why they come and what they want from the class, you will be in a better position to teach with freedom and creativity. Preparation allows your freedom and creativity to flow naturally. These aspects will definitely

make your students more at ease too! As you all grow more comfortable with one another, you will share hopes, hurts, and dreams more intimately.

(4) *E-P-I-C teaching*—This is detailed more in the chapter on Creative Teaching. However, know that this is an acrostic for Experiential, Participatory, Image Driven, and Connected (see www.leonardsweet.com). As you prepare, you'll be better able to bring many learning approaches into the teaching event. As you prepare, you'll be aware of ways you can help your students experience the text, not simply hear it or read it. Preparation helps you plan ways of involving your youth in the teaching/learning experience. Preparing brings images to your mind that you can pass on to your learners. Preparation helps you make applications of Bible truths and bring relevance to the lives of your learners. Preparation excites your students. They know you are the "real deal" where teaching the truth of Scripture is concerned. Your intentional preparation not only improves your teaching but also improves your relationships with your youth.

(5) *Sensitivity to the spiritual condition*—You will have youth in your class who have been Christians a long time. You will have youth who are new Christians or who are searching right now to know Christ. Be sensitive to the spiritual growth and development of each learner. Treat each learner individually and seek to understand how you can help each person grow in Christ. Effective teaching is as much about relationships as it is about content and methodology. Preparation will help you understand their spiritual conditions. As you prepare, you will do so with the needs of your youth in mind. As you prepare, you will understand how you can be a vessel of God in the teaching event. Your preparation will help you become a relevant teacher, a caring friend, and a spiritual guide.

(6) *Affirmation*—Take time to affirm learners. Affirmation goes a long way in motivating learners to continue their faith journeys. Frequent

affirmation keeps your learners feeling prepared for and cared for. Send birthday cards, "we missed you" cards, and celebration cards. Make periodic phone calls to check in with your class members. Take time to thank them when they do special things. Sincere affirmation, not empty praise, goes a long way in building loyalty and growing a wonderful Sunday school class. Effective preparation will help you schedule your personal time, not only your classroom time. As you prepare your teaching, you can bring in anecdotes of your students and share their successes and their interests with others. This will be a wonderful time of fellowship building as well as spiritual growth for you and your youth learners.

Prepare for Different Learning Styles

Perhaps one of the largest developing bodies of literature is that which pertains to learning styles. Scholarly research details various theories of how we learn. However, most scholars agree that people process information in three basic ways.

First, we are visual learners. We process information based on what we see. Right now you are using your sight to process the words on this page. As the words combine into thought patterns, you are "seeing" the sense of this writing. We learned visually early on through the use of flash cards and rote memory. We learned by putting symbols together even before we could read. Sight is an important part of how we learn.

The second way we process information is through auditory means. We hear words and form thoughts. Perhaps you read by "talking to yourself" the words on this page. Some people can only learn by reading out loud. We learn through what others say. What we hear is important for our learning.

The third basic way we process information is through kinesthetic means or physical activity. We learn by movement, be that moving a pencil as we take notes or moving blocks around to arrange the alphabet. We learn by playing and doing. The activities we perform in any particular setting combine with seeing and possibly hearing and enhance our ability to learn.

Works by Gardner, Kolb, Gregoric, and Belenky—to name a few—agree with the three basic ways to learn but expand these to fit their designs. Recent work by Felder and Soloman outlines eight different learning approaches, active and reflective, sensing and intuitive, visual and verbal, sequential and global. They say we process information in all eight areas at different points of a teaching/learning event.

While the majority of research has shown that most people are visual learners, most teachers tend to teach through lecture. We must do a better job of matching teaching approaches to learning preferences. Preparation helps us plan a variety of learning experiences for each class session. The following areas are suggested generally in most literature. These are meant as a basic overview of the learning styles suggested in the research.

(1) *Print*—These learners process information from reading traditional texts and doing pencil and paper exercises. Reading and writing are central to how these learners interact in the learning experience.

(2) *Visual*—Visual learners prefer slides, films, videos, demonstrations, charts, graphs, maps. They process information by observation. They like to be told "how to" do it and then learn by watching.

(3) *Auditory*—These people learn by listening. They most enjoy lectures, audiotapes, readings, and recitations. If aural learners can hear it, then they can do it.

(4) *Interactive*—Interactive learners participate in the learning event through talking. They learn best from small group experiences, discussions, debates, and question/answer sessions. They live to "share"!

(5) *Tactile*—These people process information through touching or handling. They enjoy hands-on activities, model building,

drawing, and manipulating objects. Tactile learners can best understand something if they can hold it.

(6) *Kinesthetic*—Active/player learners enjoy role-plays, drama, physical games, and the involvement of their psychomotor skills in the learning process. They learn by doing.

(7) *Olfactory*—Smeller/taster learners process information through taste or smell. When is the last time you taught using taste or smell? Be creative!

Most of us are probably not conscious of our learning preferences. However, most of us know ways we like and don't like to teach and ways we like and don't like to learn. A perceptive teacher can discern learning preferences and vary teaching to respond to preferences of the class members.

I Like to Learn

name _____

1. My favorite learning method is : (circle one)

   lecture   *small group*

   problem solving   *creative art*

2. The activity I really love is: (circle one)

   lecture   *small group*

   problem solving   *creative art*

3. The activity I really don't like is: (circle one)

   lecture   *small group*

   problem solving   *creative art*

The chart on the previous page is an elementary instrument for discovering the learning preferences of your class members. While this is not a scientific approach to discovering learning styles, it can be helpful in giving you clues to preferred learning styles. Distribute copies to your classes and ask for their feedback. This will give you insights into their individual learning preferences.

Key to the Instrument: Again, these descriptions are over-generalized and somewhat stereotypical. However, the information is shared to give the teacher a basic idea of the main types of learners and how they process information.

Lecture (Thinkers)—Those who generally prefer lecture like to think before making a connection. They need time to think and process. Thinkers are hands-on where facts and figures are concerned. They are computer-oriented and like outlines, hard data, maps, and charts. They tend to be more reflective, sensing, visual, and sequential. Thinkers can make decisions quickly if data is readily evident.

Problem Solving (Reflectors)—Those who generally prefer individual study, research, and analysis tend to be reflective. These learners need plenty of time to process information. Reflectors tend to have an "ah-ha" moment two to three weeks after your teaching. They are sensing, verbal, and global. Reflectors do not make good decisions under pressure. Ideas have to "incubate" before they translate into action.

Small Group (Feelers)—"Small group" learners live to share. Feelers process information by talking about things and interacting with others. Feelers love role-plays, brainstorming, games, and stories. They learn best by having a relaxed atmosphere and not having to make pressured decisions. Feelers tend to be active, intuitive, verbal, and global. They make decisions immediately, often trusting their intuition.

Creative Art (Doer)—Creative learners are the most kinesthetic. They learn best by doing. They process information sometimes in groups and sometimes alone, but always with activity! Doers are "hands-on"; they must see it, touch it, manipulate it, and then test it through experiments. These learners need activities on handouts that they can work with pencils. They tend to be active, sensing, visual, and sequential. Doers make decisions rather quickly if they can "work out" a comfortable solution.

Every time you teach, these four learning styles are present. All four of them exist in each individual learner! Part of your task is to discern the preferences of your class participants. Then your task is to prepare in such a way that you motivate everyone in your class to participate in the teaching/learning event. In order to include all learning styles in the class, you'll have to use three to five different teaching methods each time you teach. Proper preparation will keep your teaching from getting in a rut and become stale and less than challenging.

Five Guidelines for Effective Teaching

Five guidelines lead to teaching excellence. These guidelines help you stay focused on quality Bible teaching and quality people touching. Your preparation will insure that you are doing everything possible to be ready when learners come to you.

(1) *The Bible is the main textbook.* Curriculum materials guide the study. The Bible is our guide for life. The Bible is the most important spiritual book in our lives. In Bible teaching events, the Bible is the only textbook. Classes do not vote on this. This is not open for discussion! How can we do Bible study if we don't use the Bible?

Curriculum materials are guides for moving us through a consistent study of the Bible. Curriculum is not the text; it is not a sourcebook of truth. The study materials are resources for aiding our study. Curriculum materials insure a comprehensive study of the Bible over a consistent period of time.

Consider the following analogy: Think of the Bible as a large, beautiful swimming pool. In the typical youth Bible study, the available time given to teach a particular lesson limits you from swimming in the entire pool! How do you get in the pool? How do you get to the areas of need for the class?

Curriculum materials act as the diving board to get us into the pool. Bounce upon the board a few times, get a feel for the passage in relation to the whole of Scripture, and then dive in! Once you are in the pool, swim to wherever you need to go to meet the needs of your class. There is no way you can teach the whole Bible from Genesis to Revelation in one class session. Likewise, don't feel that you have to teach every verse of the lesson passage. Teach to meet needs. Enjoy swimming with friends!

Bo shares a recent teaching encounter. "I recently greeted one of our teachers in the hallway. She was near tears. She said to me in a shaky voice, 'For the first time as a Sunday school teacher, I failed. I just couldn't cover the entire lesson!'

'What happened?' I asked, truly concerned for my friend.

'Well, Tonya was back today for the first Sunday since her dad died. As we began the class I asked her how she was doing, and she started crying. Her sadness upset the rest of my girls. So we spent most of the entire teaching time crying and praying and hugging Tonya. I'm so sorry, I just couldn't teach after that!'

I hugged her and said, 'My understanding of teaching is such that you probably taught your greatest Sunday school lesson today! Thank you!'

We both walked away a bit more affirmed in the love of Christ and reminded of what happens when we come together for sharing. What a wonderful picture of what teaching is actually about!"

(2) *The teacher is the guide; the student must want to participate.* As a teacher of youth, you are not responsible for the learning of your students. You are the "tour guide" along the learning journey.

Your challenge is to engage your youth in such a way that they want to join in the learning experience. One way we engage the learner is through the use of a variety of teaching methods. The next chapter is filled with ideas and suggestions for creative teaching.

Another way to engage the learner is to know the needs, struggles, and joys of your youth. Youth teaching happens as much out of the church as it does in your classroom. Go to where your youth are. Visit them in their homes. Participate in their extracurricular activities. See them in their day-to-day environments. As you see them in these places, you'll come to understand better their spiritual joys and struggles. As you teach to meet needs, you will show yourself to be a relevant guide. Your youth will appreciate your efforts and respond.

One other way to motivate your youth is for you to be an authentic Christian with them. As a Christian, if you are not transparent with your learners, they will perceive you as a fake! The one thing youth can discern quickly is insincerity; if they perceive this in you, they'll not participate. Youth need to know that you struggle in your faith. Youth need to know the lessons you've learned as a growing Christian. Youth need you to model for them the "joy and the pain" of authentic faith.

(3) *The teacher is a mentor, not a "buddy"!* You are not a youth; you are an adult. Youth need to see you as a growing and mature Christian. Yes, they need you to relate to them. Yes, youth need you to sometimes speak their language and sometimes be clued in to their culture. Youth do not need you to be one of them! Youth today need positive role models, mentors who will guide and shape them.

There will be times when you can be wild and crazy with your youth. They need to see your natural personality emerge. They need honest and open communication with you. They need you to be yourself, to let your personality emerge. But you will walk a fine line as you work with youth. I've known many youth workers in my years of ministry. Those who were most effective were those who knew when to be "youthful" and when to be mentor. Pray for guidance. Pay attention to your actions. Lead with confidence.

(4) *Teach to share information and lead to transformation.* Youth are active learners. They do not learn well by sitting still and listening to content. Too often we try to tell youth everything they need to know about spiritual matters. Sharing content is a different approach than teaching for transformation.

Transformational learning means we allow youth opportunities to test out their faith. Transformational learning means we offer information and then dialogue and share opinions. As we interact and play and study, sometimes youth ask the hard questions. They expect us to deal openly and honestly with those questions.

(5) *Planning is crucial!* You cannot bluff your way through teaching youth for too many Sundays. The landscape of youth needs is too complicated. The needs of youth are too important for us to fly by the seats of our pants! Youth need teachers who are prepared each and every Sunday morning. Youth need teachers who have planned an exciting, interactive learning experience. Youth need teachers who care enough to plan and prepare and present in ways that communicate sincere efforts at guiding the learning event. The following outline is a suggested approach for individual study and preparation. However, do not neglect the synergy that comes from planning with your other teachers as well.

A Weekly Preparation Plan

As you prepare each week, a good plan of study is critical. As you study, one important aspect is to give the information time to soak in your soul. The following suggestions will help you grow as a teacher and as a disciple:

Here are a few tools that should be near your place of preparation. The knowledgeable teacher always prepares with the following:

(1) *Bible*—The Bible is the textbook for your study. Read the study passage in several different translations during the week. Become a student of the Bible, not just a processor of information.

(2) *Class roll*—As you prepare each week, do so with the names of your class members in front of you. Keep their names in your conscious mind as you study and prepare.

(3) *Pen and notepad or notebook*—As you prepare each week, lessons and ideas will flood your mind. You cannot possibly remember all the ideas that will come to you. Take notes. You will also be challenged by ideas with which you need to wrestle personally. Again, jot down notes and continue to grow in your spiritual life.

The following outline has proven effective for me over the years. This is a daily plan for intentional preparation. It helps you avoid the temptation of cramming the night before. An intentional and disciplined approach to preparation will help you grow as a teacher and as a Bible learner. Remember that most of our teaching comes from the overflow of our study. Preparation that follows this model will enhance your presentation.

Sunday Evening (20 minutes)—Read the main Scripture passage for the coming week's lesson. Evaluate how your last teaching session went. Think about the individual and collective needs of your class in relation to this passage. Perhaps read the passage in several translations and jot down key words or ideas. Pray for your class members, class prospects, and their families.

Monday (20 minutes)—Read the entire Bible passage for the lesson. Try to get a feel for the larger section of Scripture that contains your main study passage. Read through Bible background and commentary notes as well as your teaching materials that relate to the passage. Highlight truths relevant to the needs of your class. Make notes if applicable. Pray for the central points of your presentation to be made clear to you as you study.

Tuesday (20 minutes)—Read the suggested teaching procedures. Make notes or highlight methods you think will be effective with your class and their learning styles. Identify effective opening and closing activities for the class session. Pray for your class needs and for other teachers and church leaders.

Wednesday (20 minutes)—Develop a three- or four-point outline about the teaching material. Think about ways to motivate study, examine the Scripture, and apply the Bible to life.

Identify one thought you want to make sure you communicate this week. Jot down other key words or thoughts that will help you teach and communicate with clarity. Focus your teaching on that one thought and how you can supplement other truths around this. Pray for guidance in formulating the teaching plan.

Thursday (30 minutes)—Begin working toward a final teaching outline with appropriate teaching ideas for each point. You should work to limit your outline to three or four main points. Identify and finalize teaching procedures for attaining maximum class participation. Make a list of special materials that will support your teaching. Pray for your plans and those who will study with you this Sunday.

Friday, Saturday, Sunday (as needed)—Review your teaching notes and outline. Be confident in the teaching methods you will use. Perhaps practice your lecture material. (Remember that lectures should be no longer than eight minutes at one time.) Gather all needed supplies. Pray each day for the teaching/learning experience you will lead.

Develop each lesson with a balance of emotional content and informational content. In each lesson, be sure to include moments for inspiration and motivation. Make sure you direct youth to Scripture examination, looking up the text in the Bible and reading from the

Bible. In closing each lesson, challenge the class to incorporate one new learning idea into their lives for the coming week. Pray daily and apply yourself in study and preparation.

There is nothing better you can do for yourself or your students than to prepare. The more you prepare, the more confident you'll become. Your task is to present the material openly, honestly, and with a "prepared for and cared for" attitude. Allow the youth learners opportunities for discovery and personal interaction. Finally, leave the results to God. You'll be a great teacher! You'll be pleasantly surprised at what God does through you.

Chapter Five

Creative Teaching—More than Telling, Selling, or Yelling

Teaching youth used to be so easy! In the good old days, young people came eagerly with other family members to Sunday school. They came to grow in spiritual maturity; they came to study the Bible seriously; they came for inspiration and fellowship. They sat still and listened; we instilled the information we knew they needed. They "sat still" while we "instilled" what we had "distilled" through preparation and experience. Ah, teaching was simpler, less complicated, and pressure free. Yeah, right!

Sadly, many churches still think teaching youth is a "you sit still and I'll instill" approach. Many youth Sunday school teachers stand near the podium and deliver their "sermon" for the week. Many youth teachers have no idea of the world these teenagers now experience. They simply point their fingers, holler Bible verses, and expect youth to respond with a "kum-bah-yah" affirmation. However, effective teaching is far more than simply "telling, selling, or yelling."

Youth today come to us for a variety of reasons. Their expectations are high about what church should be doing. Youth today leave their high-technology homes filled with high-technology inventions. Their bedrooms have the technology to connect them with friends around the world in the twinkling of an eye. They generally come to church in their own cars (rarely do they come with their parents) filled with high-tech gadgets. They come in designer clothes, from designer homes, looking for challenge, inspiration, and interaction.

We usher them into our less than state-of-the-art classrooms. Most Sunday school rooms are no more than paneled or concrete block walls and carpet that was there fifty years ago. None of us would have carpet in our homes for fifty years! We pay little or no attention to the physical environment that affects our learning. Yet, youth are used to state-of-the-art learning experiences.

We pay even less attention to the emotional and intellectual environment of Sunday school. We tell them what they need to know with little emotion. We sell them on the aspects of Christianity, especially the need to sacrifice, abstain, and "live right." We yell at them and dump guilt on them. We shake our heads because they don't bring their Bibles, don't study their lessons, and don't seem committed.

We forget, however, that we are there to guide them on the pathway. We forget that we are there to make the Gospel story inviting and energizing. We forget the models Jesus gave us for reaching, teaching, and loving!

The ability to teach young people biblical truths is crucial to helping them grow and mature as followers of Christ. As teachers, we present challenges, information, and inspiration week after week. We have immediate access to the resources that enhance our teaching. The Internet, interactive commentaries, and other Bible resource support are readily available for teaching preparation and presentation. We have to know our learners, know about our learners, and "bear up" their lives as we teach and lead.

Good teachers know they can no longer "bluff" their way through a lesson. Effective and challenging teaching approaches are much needed in today's church. Why, then, do so many teachers teach with little or no preparation? Why do so many teachers use poor teaching methods? Why do so many teachers refuse to contact class members and prospects? Why are so many teachers lazy in their teaching assignment?

Possibly, some teachers don't understand the dedication needed to teach youth. Perhaps many teachers are too busy in their weekly schedules. Probably, most of our teachers are dedicated to teaching youth but need fresh teaching ideas to keep themselves and their classes engaged. All of those who teach need consistent training, resources, and helps.

By blending traditional teaching methods with innovative approaches, Sunday school can be fun, inspirational, and relational. As we blend traditional methods of Sunday school ministry with innovative and creative approaches for the twenty-first century, we open ourselves to be used more effectively by the Lord. As we make ourselves more open to God, we position ourselves to build community and maybe impact our world!

Stuff 'em!

A favorite humorous quote on teaching is "The sign of a good teacher is one who knows their stuff, knows who they're stuffing, and stuffs 'em real good!" While this usually gets a few laughs, the point is serious. Teaching is more than "stuffing 'em real good"!

Can you imagine a preschool or children's Sunday school class where all the students sit quietly while the teacher lectures for an hour? How ridiculous is that? We know that preschoolers and children are active learners. They learn best in an environment that stimulates their senses and encourages them to explore. The lecture method does not work well in this environment.

Actually, the lecture method is not the most effective teaching method with any age group! The most effective teaching method is the method that involves the learners in the teaching/learning process. The least effective teaching method is the one you use all the time! Teach with creativity and variety. Teach to help youth learners discover truths for themselves. There is nothing like the joy of seeing the truth dawn on them.

As you teach youth, plan your lesson around three to five different teaching approaches during a class session. Discussion, brainstorming, creative writing, music, and even a dash of drama keep the learning environment lively. Fun food is always good for livening up discussion or rewarding participation. Don't get too "cute" with the exercises, but let Bible learning be fun, interactive, and thought provoking. You are in control of the classroom. Plan for maximum results from each teaching opportunity.

The lecture method, if done well, is an appropriate and effective teaching method. When you lecture to youth, do so in short blocks. Never lecture for more than ten minutes. Break your lecture into "chunks" of information using different activities to emphasize your information. Youth today are not linear in their thinking. They make application by "clumping" different thoughts together. Break up your lecturing with "clumps" of application and interactive methods.

Plan your teaching session in blocks using a variety of teaching methods. Decide what are the two or three most important truths or challenges that you wish to convey. Let these be the pillars around which you build your lecture. Then supplement your lecture with a time for questions and sharing to bring impact to the teaching.

Allow youth ample time to interact and share their thoughts with one another. They need to interact with one another, to hear what their friends are thinking. You need to hear their thoughts too. Guide the learning experience to include all who are in the room. Structure your teaching so that the class hears your comments and thoughts, but seek balance between your presentation time and their interaction time. (See the preceding chapter on "Preparation.")

Teach to help youth think critically, to examine the Bible and decide for themselves what God is saying to people. Help youth decide what God is saying to each learner individually too. Don't make the mistake of trying to tell the class participants everything they need to know. Guide them to make exciting discoveries on their own. Self-discovery learning is fun, motivational, and exciting. For too long we have lectured to impart information. The most effective teaching moves from information to maturity and transformation.

Activity-oriented learning also has higher retention rates, especially for youth and adult learners. Find creative and interactive ways to present materials. Find ways to teach lesson materials so learners can discuss information together. Teaching, when it is done best, is relational and fosters sharing.

A favorite prayer sentence is "Help me remember, Lord, that all the truth I know is not all the truth!" Effective teachers build upon the experiences of their youth learners. Today's youth have a rich variety of learning experiences. Allow them time to share with one another. Allow them time to play and be silly. Allow them time to be serious and seek God's guidance. As we share with each other in the class, we learn and grow together.

Jesus modeled interactive teaching. He used a variety of teaching methods—sometimes stories, sometimes humor, sometimes question-and-answer, and sometimes lecture. His preparation was built upon the experiences of the learners around him. As a wise and prepared teacher, he was sensitive to the teachable moment and flexible enough to balance a variety of teaching methods. Jesus was a creative, inspiring, and motivating instructor. He was molding a community of learners into friends. He was preparing his followers to become servants of God. So are we.

Nine Helps for Teaching

The following nine guidelines will help you build toward meaningful teaching and learning in the classroom.

(1) *Give youth opportunities to participate in the learning experience.* Passive learning does not grow learners effectively. Active learning allows all who are present to learn from one another. Youth learners enjoy talking with one another and learning from one another. Youth learn best when they are involved in the teaching/learning event.

(2) *Give youth opportunities to apply lesson truths to their individual lives.* Youth learners today are conditioned to instant feedback. They expect to be "graded" on their learning. To keep learner motivation high, provide immediate feedback and affirmation. Tell youth when their ideas are on track. Help them see and understand where they may be misunderstanding something. Guide them as they form their own spiritual lives. Relevant and practical experiences, for all age

groups, will make a difference in their interest and consistent attendance.

(3) *Give youth opportunities to understand the big picture of Scripture.* Too often we emphasize short segments of Scripture. We spotlight Bible stories or Bible truths but fail to show how these fit into the bigger story of redemption. We even encourage memorization of Bible verses with little or no application. From time to time, remind learners how these "small pieces" relate to the total picture of God's redemptive love. Jesus summed up the whole of God's work in these two para- phrased commandments: "Love God with all your heart, soul, and mind, with all of your being, and love your neighbor as much as you love yourself." Occasionally, we need to remind learners how the little parts fit together.

(4) *Give youth priority attention in the classroom.* Be "learner-oriented" and "teacher-flexible." The teaching/learning process begins when the first young person arrives. The teacher should always arrive first and be ready. Teach with youth in mind. Sometimes your ideas may be great adult ideas; if so, try to relate the idea to a youth orientation. Teach to keep the learning environment open, involving, and exciting.

(5) *Give youth opportunities for honest sharing in a climate of honesty and safety.* Youth need to know first that they won't get laughed at our ridiculed. They absolutely will not share until they feel safe. Building trust takes time. Ask lighthearted questions as class begins and go deeper as trust grows.

Innovative Sunday school classes allow for times of laughter and tears. Exciting Bible teaching allows for fun and for serious interac- tion. Use positive examples of humor, use honest life illustrations, and be open to the leadership of God's spirit in the growth, maturity, and intimacy of your class.

(6) *Check your ego at the door.* An ineffective teacher can ruin an exciting learning experience. An ego-driven teacher can squelch

interaction and relational learning. A controlling teacher can stifle relationship building and spiritual growth. You are not the judge of these young learners; you are their guide. If you come across too heavy-handed, they will turn you off. You are not the coolest person in the room; you are their friend. If you come across too "youth-oriented," they will not trust you.

Trust your prayer life to guide you toward the truths that will directly impact your class. Don't be afraid to say to your class, "I don't know . . . but I will find out!" Openness and honesty go far in building a loving and accepting Sunday school class.

(7) *Be creative as a teacher.* Be prepared and caring. Be flexible. These actions will go far to help you grow as you lead youth. We all want to be challenged with the excitement of biblical truths. Youth especially want to build a strong faith foundation that will serve them well as they grow. In our teenage years, most of us begin to understand what being a follower of Christ means. What you teach and how you teach will impact your youth learners for the rest of their lives!

(8) *Be confident in the power of Christ.* Enter every teaching opportunity filled with confidence that you have done your best each week to open yourself to the loving power of God. Teach with confidence and sensitivity. Leave the results to God! You are the messenger; God is the message. As you teach with attentiveness both to the Holy Spirit and to the youth learners, you can be assured that blessings and miracles will abound.

(9) *Have fun!* Too often we forget that learning is fun. Your youth like to be active, interactive, and sometimes silly. If learning isn't fun and meaningful, youth will turn you off and tune you out. Laugh out loud from time to time.

Creative Teaching Ideas

Teaching with a variety of methods brings excitement to our classrooms. We can electrify our learning environment with a little effort. Remember, we don't have to overload the senses of our classes every week. You are planning for three to five different teaching methods in a class session. Know the needs of your class and the pace at which they like to learn.

You have to begin the teaching journey by teaching. Trial and error is a wonderful teacher. If your class knows you are prepared for them and you care about them, they will give you grace as you discover your confidence.

The best way to learn what works is to try something new. Yes, you might be uncomfortable at first. Yes, the youth might give you a little grief and be slow to respond, but they will participate if you lead with confidence. Practice, practice, practice! Involve your learners, have fun, and let the learning soar. The depth of your learning experiences will amaze you. With a little practice and lots of preparation, you will become an exciting and interactive teacher. You may even witness a miracle happening through those wonderful chunky crayons or another verse of "Kum-bah-yah"!

The following teaching approaches are ideas to help you add creativity to your teaching. (A longer checklist appears at the end of this chapter. Make sure you choose variety in your teaching. See also Appendix A.)

(1) *Paper/pencil/print*—Brainstorming lists, true/false responses, fill-in-the-blank questions, word search puzzles, hangman, and many more help enhance learning.

Youth respond well to reading and writing. Invite learners to read out loud from the Bible. Ask them to share inspirational poems or share texts from other readings to amplify the lesson. Guide them to practice "rewriting" Scripture passages in their own words.

(2) *Visual*—These materials include videos, computers, charts, maps, posters—more than simply a printed page or a crayon activity. Show short clips of a video (three to five minutes in length; not a baby-sitting tool or a way to pass time). Use charts, maps, and posters to elaborate your teaching points. Expand learner attention with a demonstration or brief dramatic presentation.

(3) *Audio*—Audiotapes, computer-generated sounds, dramatic readings, and lectures expand the teaching tools at our disposal. Introduce a new unit of study with a Bible character sharing insights. Play an audiotape clip (again no longer than five minutes) to add to the teaching. Enlist class members prior to class to assist in a dramatic reading or vocal choir. Again, remember, when you lecture, do so in short "chunks" no more than eight to ten minutes at a time. Supplement your lectures with other teaching methods.

(4) *Touch or Tactile*—Youth love hands-on activities. Drawing and coloring, pencil and paper activities, model building, and manipulating objects are ways to expand your teaching. Let your learners "touch" the Bible and excite their learning. Let them feel the smooth texture of anointing oil, let them feel the roughness of a "solid" rock, let them touch lamb's wool.

Give them pipe cleaners, paper cups, or construction paper and have them mold these into visual metaphors. Give them modeling clay or chunky crayons and let them do art projects. Lead them to hold their Bibles and find obscure verses for reference. Play "spin the bottle" (not for kisses) to see who has to answer the next question.

The more objects with which youth can interact, the more they will learn. The more objects with which youth can interact, the more they will remember. As they learn and remember, they will grow in applying Bible truths to their lives.

(5) *Personal Interaction*—Small group experiences, discussion/question-and-answer sessions, debate, and sharing times allow for more

creative approaches to Bible teaching. Youth are especially motivated when sharing their thoughts and opinions with others.

Youth are riding an emotional roller coaster. As we teach them, there will be times when they react with great emotion and not understand why. As we guide them to deal honestly with their emotions, we help them learn how to express themselves appropriately. The young Jesus also had to learn to express his emotions appropriately. Teach with sensitivity and compassion and help youth grow in an emotional and spiritual maturity that will serve them well into adulthood.

Youth are relationship driven. If their friends come to Sunday school, they will come. If their friends participate and interact, they will do so too. Friendships are crucial to the learning of youth. Friendships with their peers and their teachers are important. Youth need to know that they can come to a safe place and be in a safe environment. They need to know that the friendships they make will serve them well in their learning and growth. As youth grow in and learn from friends, they also learn about themselves, their God, and God's word. There is joy in seeing a young, timid sixth grader grow in wisdom and stature and develop into a mature, responsible young adult.

(6) *Activity Learning*—Active learning is that which uses our psychomotor skills. Standing up and moving around, clapping our hands, drawing, acting, games, and more help break up the monotony of sitting and listening for a lesson. As we get the blood flowing to the brain, we stimulate the learner. Get them up and moving around! As you do, learning is strengthened and remembered.

Youth learn by doing. They love to let their imaginations run wild. They are stimulated by doing and then discussing. Youth enjoy being involved in planning, doing, and evaluating the learning processes. Activity-oriented learning with youth allows for a depth of discussion and interaction. Activity-oriented learning allows for a depth of spiritual searching and growth. What a great experience to see a young person have an "aha!" moment in their spiritual growth.

(7) *Taste and Smell*—This approach brings the learner into the world of the Bible. Eating and drinking foods of the Bible are a great approach. When you talk about salt and light, remind learners of salt (or of no salt!). Foods from Bible lands are readily available today.

(8) *Music*—Rather than falling under "Audio," music is an area all its own. We don't use music enough in our class experiences. Scripture invites us to "make a joyful noise" as praise to God. Preschoolers and children love singing. Somehow, as we get older, we forget the joy (and the learning) that can come from singing. Find ways to spice up your teaching with music. Excite the learner, inspire the learner, sing!

(9) *Concrete, Abstract, and Application*—Youth are at the age and stage to think both in a concrete way and an abstract way. Youth can concretely express their faith. They can also conceptualize models for faith expression. Don't be frustrated as a teacher and don't frustrate youth learners by locking in on one way of teaching. Youth love variety. They love activity. Find ways to present lesson truths in a variety of teaching methods. Allow youth to express themselves in concrete and abstract ways. The youth of today are some of the most gifted and talented people in history! Give these talented people freedom to explore, to grow, and to develop into wonderfully gifted Christians.

Youth learners are looking for life application. Yes, they need excitement, interaction, and a variety of approaches. But youth learners also need to see and feel how the biblical message applies to their lives. Be fun in your teaching; youth certainly want to enjoy the process. Above all, though, offer practical application for their lives. As you guide youth to meaning and truth, you enable them to grow to become leaders in your church and God's kingdom!

When using a variety of learning activities with youth, state the time limit you allow for a particular experience. For instance, "For the next three minutes, we're going to listen to an audiotape of . . . ." Or "For the next five minutes, I want you to work in small groups to . . . ." The reason for this disclaimer is to help youth relax. Some learners may not enjoy the particular learning approach, but all of us can endure and enjoy a three- to five-minute learning experience.

An interactive person will understand that you are not going to lecture for an hour. A shy person will understand that the small group experience will not last forever. A thinking person will hear that we aren't going to play games for the entire class session. Remember, people go where they know they've been prepared for and are cared for. As we give them time limits for the variety of teaching methods, we let learners know that we have prepared for them and that we care for them.

E-P-I-C Teaching

Leonard Sweet uses the acrostic "E-P-I-C" to challenge teachers to make more interesting and engaging presentations (see www.leonardsweet.com). In *Building Blocks for Sunday School Growth*, authors Bo Prosser, Michael McCullar, and Charles Qualls challenge teachers to use three to five teaching methods for each Sunday school teaching session. Think about using a variety of teaching methods that would embrace each of these "EPIC" areas as you prepare and present your lessons.

E: Experiential—Too many of us simply teach "content" to those who come to our Sunday school classes. Teaching that is "informational" does little more than present "facts" to the youth learner. Teenagers' lives are filled with rich experiences of faith and growth. Spend a few moments watching television commercials. You'll soon discover that advertisers are not selling products anymore. They are selling experiences. Watch and you'll see advertisements for a motorcycle experience, an eating experience, and a vacation experience. What kind of "experience" are you presenting as you teach?

Experiential teaching is "transformational" and helps youth grow in the faith. Give your youth a learning experience that lets them "feel," "do," or "think" in relation to the Bible passage. Give your youth a communal experience that lets them interact with one another and builds friendships. Give your youth a spiritual experience that leads them into relationship with the living God.

P: Participatory—Surfing the Internet is a participatory experience. Ebay.com and Amazon.com are interactive and demand a response. Many youth who come to your teaching event have surfed the Net before coming. My daughter has been known to carry on fourteen or more IM's (instant messages) at one time! The study of God's word should also be participatory. We learn much more when we share our experiences and our thoughts. Again, use three to five teaching methods in a session.

Give youth learners time to reflect and do something in response to information you share and challenges you issue. We all want participatory learning experiences. As we participate in the learning experience, we begin to internalize the truth of the teaching event rather than be "entertained" by the event.

I: Image Driven—A picture is worth a thousand words or maybe even more! Someone once said that the mind never thinks without a picture. An image, an object, a tangible expression of a Bible truth gives a much deeper emphasis than our words alone. Each week as you teach, find an image/picture/object to help you emphasize your points. Warning: The image must have relevance to the teaching event.

The Internet is a valuable resource in helping you find image-rich teaching helps. Most of us think in pictures. You will discover a rich resource of free pictures/images/objects to lead your students to even deeper thoughts and growth (for example, www.freeimages.com; www.freefoto.com; www.webshots.com.)

Think of how much images impact your life. A bright yellow pair of arches (McDonald's), a bright red circle with white script (Coca Cola), the "swoosh" (Nike), the peacock (NBC television), the old man with a string bowtie (Kentucky Fried Chicken), an orange and black cartoon tiger (Kellogg's Frosted Flakes). How many more can you think of? Needless to say, we are an image-rich society. Bring this visual dimension into your teaching.

C: Connected—Too many Sunday school classes are taught with little or no attention paid to the application of the lesson material. There is a disconnection between the words of "then" and the living of "now." Teaching with connectedness is difficult. To be connected means we must know our learners' needs. Being connected assumes that we know what's happening in the lives of our class members. Connected, relevant teaching challenges the teacher to be more than just a "talking head." Connected teaching means preparing for and caring for the people in our classes.

I can sit in my home and operate a computer in Washington State that communicates with a satellite and operates a live camera around the world (see www.earthcam.com as one example.) I can communicate instantly with a friend serving in Afghanistan. The world is now a fairly small community. The church exists to connect us to God and to connect us to one another. Youth especially are feeling "disconnected" from peers, from parents, and from God. Teach with connectedness to bring meaning into the learning event.

Good Teaching Never Stops

Your job as a growing teacher never stops. There are always more images to download, websites to explore, commentaries to read, and youth to reach. There will never be enough time to get it all done. The good news for you is that you don't have to be an expert presenter.

The challenge is to be an engaging and energetic teacher. As you share your learning experiences in a variety of ways, you'll grow as a better teacher. As you share your learning experiences with energy, you'll grow as a better teacher. As you share your learning experiences with relevance, you'll grow as a better teacher. Practice, practice, practice!

The chart on the next page is offered as a beginning source of teaching techniques. It is not meant to be exhaustive. Try to use three

Creative Teaching Techniques (see also Appendix A)

Have fun using a variety of creative teaching techniques in your presentations.

Listening, Discussing, Reporting
Lecture *(eight to ten minutes at a time)*
Formal and informal discussions
Question and answer *(use open ended questions; nothing that can be answered "yes" or "no")*
Brainstorming ideas and solutions
Short report writing
Debating
Storytelling with questions
Outlines and handouts
Facts and figures reporting
Maps and charts
Improvisation *(good for telling group stories one word at a time)*
Buzz groups
Case study interactions
Memorization and reporting
Book reviews
Lesson overviews or summaries
Dramatic readings
Strategic listening
Scavenger hunts
Puzzles
Group praying

Writing, Doing, Using Paper/Pencils
Word search
Crossword puzzles
Word games
Book/Bible scavenger hunts
Fill-in-the-blank questions
Story writing
Paraphrasing Scripture passages
True/false questions
Matching and multiple-choice questions
Note-taking
Creative writing
Interviewing (in a journalistic style)
Questionnaires
Concordance and Bible dictionary searches
Letter writing
Writing prayers
Think–do–reflect activities
Journaling

Interactive, Active Learning, Sharing
Singing in groups and solos
Small group interacting
Story writing and sharing
Multimedia presentations
Drama and role-playing
Experimenting
Hymn reading, singing, and writing
Interviewing (person-on-the-street approach)
Charades and other low-level competitive games
Pictionary™ and drawing games
Movie and video clips
Arts and crafts activities
Computer-oriented learning
Cartooning
Praying
Reading aloud
Sound and action games

For more on creative teaching, see Bo Prosser with Michael McCullar and Charles Qualls, *Building Blocks for Sunday School Growth* (Macon: Smyth & Helwys, 2002).

to five different teaching techniques for each class. You'll make your teaching more fun, and your youth will thank you for risking. (For more helps on teaching techniques and presentation skills, see www.amazon.com; www.youthlearn.org; www.teachingtechniques.com; www.helwys.com)

Chapter Six

Outreach and Inreach

Once upon a time, before the car was a convenience owned by nearly every family, the activities of the community revolved around the church. Sunday mornings were a time for the community to gather at the house of worship and share time together at Sunday school and "Big Church." The community even returned for Sunday night worship. The church was not just a building in the community; it was the centerpiece. People took care of each other through prayer, worship, cooking, and watching each other's children. It was a different time. Your biggest choice was deciding what denomination you were, even though your parents or marriage partner usually made that choice for you. The next big decision was what you would wear. Notice that the decision was not whether you would go! This all changed one day for a host of reasons.

Today church is different. People drive for miles to attend the church of their choice. The first decision they face is not which church to attend, but whether to choose church over coffee and bagels at the local coffeehouse. However, this chapter is not about the reasons people choose whether or not to attend church. This chapter is about the church's responsibility to reach the community and give them a reason to join a fellowship. More specifically, it is about the role Sunday school must play in this process.

Outreach and inreach provide people the opportunity to connect with a set of others who can become their chosen family, their friends, and even their network of support. Outreach and inreach offer ways to help people connect with a community of faith that will assist them in their spiritual growth. If the church is to thrive, its members must be focused on connecting with the community and ultimately with God. What better place for this to happen than through Sunday school!

The Great Commission

Go therefore in the world, baptizing all nations. —Matthew 28:19-20

Believe it or not, God calls the church to do outreach. Outreach is not simply on Sunday morning after the service when you welcome a new member to church. Outreach is the process that helps a person or family come to a point where they join the church or make a profession of faith. Through the Great Commission, God commands the church to be inclusive, reaching all people, not exclusive in its membership. Throughout the New Testament, Jesus develops the disciples but preaches to the community. His mission is not only about the Twelve.

The shift in many churches today has been for the worship service to be the front door of the church. While worship is a wonderful avenue into the church, I am reminded of an old doormat that used to sit at my grandmother's back door: "Back door friends are the best." Worship as outreach is passive at best, ineffective at worst. Sunday school as outreach is active and part of the Great Commission. Outreach through Sunday school incorporates people into the life of your church through relationships, small groups, and niches. When was the last time you entered a room full of people at a party or conference and became excited that you did not know anyone? Face it—small groups make great locations to involve people in the life of the church.

In the introduction to this chapter, I noted that people went to church on Sundays when the church was the center of the community. Recognizing this as a blanket statement, note that in today's consumer culture, people generally do not simply come to church anymore. Several years ago, my wife and I left a church in one town at which I was employed. We moved for her job to another town. I was excited about the opportunity to visit churches and experience them as an outsider rather than as a new staff person. What I found was that we made convenient excuses not to attend church on several occasions. When we did attend, we were either discreet, or people there did not notice us. Only two churches made follow-up contacts, and today we are members of one of those two. The one we chose invited us to Sunday school and had someone to greet us who guided us through the building. The point is that people do not simply go to church anymore. Many see no reason, while others seek a reason but do not often find it. Church is not the same institution it was a century ago when the agricultural community held Sunday sacred. People do not attend because "it is the right thing to do." Considering these facts, why do people attend or visit a new church in a new community? The single biggest factor is relationships: with God and with others. This is why Sunday school must do outreach.

The Shape of Outreach: H.E.A.R.T.

H:Heart—Outreach must begin with a Christian spirit of love and caring that lends reason to placing a phone call or inviting someone to Sunday school. A minister was once asked, "Why do you do what you do?" His answer was simple but insightful: "I do what I do to honor the saints who went before me." Before you think his answer was based on some odd commitment to St. Augustine or St. Francis, let me describe the saints to whom he referred. A saint is the sweet little lady who taught you the great Bible stories accompanied by apple juice and butter cookies. A saint is the patient man who took you and your classmates camping in the rain. A saint is the youth volunteer who loved you when you couldn't love yourself. You see, church, Sunday school, and outreach are not just for you. They are for reaching others, telling the stories of God, and loving the unlovable. Reach out for the saints. Be a saint.

E:Enabled—A second facet of outreach is how empowered or enabled you are to do outreach. Some people are not aware of how to do outreach or even why they should do it. You have already read about the "why"; the how is coming. You are a vital part of the life of your church and your class. You have been called by God to reach out to others around you, whether they are your classmates, coworkers, neighbors, or visitors to the church. Do not wait on a staff member or teacher to give you the authority to make contacts or extend invitations to people. Your authority comes from the instructions of God.

A:Allegience—Outreach would be popular if it were always easy or required little time. In a later section of this chapter, you will read about tools and ideas to help simplify systematic outreach practices for you and your class. Recognize that to implement these ideas or any others you create takes a commitment of time and energy. Some prospects take several months and even years to make a final decision to join a church or Sunday school group. Are you willing to continue to cultivate relationships regardless of the time it may take?

Before you dismiss outreach due to the time and commitment it takes, remember this: Outreach begins with you. Inviting your classmate, coworker, friend, or new neighbor to join you at church takes less time than reading this paragraph. Everyone has time to do that much. Following up with visitors and prospects of the church takes a little more time. Coordinating outreach for your class takes a little more. Regardless of which you choose to do, they all take a commitment.

R:Routine—A coordinated effort by a Sunday school class takes not only a commitment, but also a routine. That routine includes a plan and consistency from volunteers. What type of plan will you develop? Perhaps your plan will include some of the tools from this chapter. It may be a creation of your design or a hybrid of both. Determine your plan and be ready to move forward. Your next step is to recruit volunteers who will be committed to assisting in the plan. Once you do these things, be consistent. Follow up on a weekly basis with prospects rather than doing so once a quarter. If you wait too long you might communicate a lack of caring or concern for the prospect.

Be consistent with what you ask your volunteers to do and to say. Give them a script or a list of questions to follow and ask during an initial phone call contact. Be honest with prospects about your class. Do not tell them what you think they want to hear. Your class may or may not prove to be a good fit for a certain individual. The sooner this is realized, the better chance you have to help someone assimilate into a class that better fits his or her needs.

T:Time—Despite the many technological and digital tools that promise to help us save time, there are still only twenty-four hours in a day and seven days in a week. Anytime you take on a new project or commitment, assess the time it will take and whether or not you have time available. Outreach does not have to be done at one specific time or through one specific medium. The telephone is still the single greatest tool available for doing outreach. A call takes only a few minutes. You may not be comfortable with this method, so what other options are available to you? Be creative. Many guest information cards now ask for email addresses. You can compose and send emails anytime of the day or night. Imagine how delighted you would be to receive a "howdy" in your inbox from the church you just visited as opposed to spam from yet another generic drug company. You may recognize a prospect from your daughter's soccer league or from your son's school. Make the opportunity to connect with these people at those venues. Your time is precious. Your opportunities to connect with people are too numerous for them not to fit into your schedule somehow.

How-tos of Outreach

This section is a sample outreach plan you might use. Please note that not all activities and ideas are right for your church or community, but the basic ideas are the same. Adapt, create, and have fun finding the best ways that you and your students can do outreach at your church.

Every team needs a coach. The first step in developing a plan is to find someone who will be a capable and committed leader for the outreach ministry of your class. You may find that a student can do the job well, but always have an adult advisor. Also be careful about assigning the job to someone whose tendencies are early excitement but little organization or follow through.

(1) *Build the team.* Recruiting volunteers for a project can be one of the most tedious and frustrating tasks. For outreach in your class, educate adult volunteers, parents, and the youth on why outreach is important. Remind them of God's call to reach others. Most importantly, spend time in prayer, asking God to create hearts for outreach in your class. Be specific about job requirements. This may involve developing job descriptions. A sample description would include the mission (this team may develop its own mission statement) of the outreach ministry, time requirements, and job requirements (phone calls, follow-up notes, outreach activities, meeting times, etc.).

(2) *Recruit people for tasks at which they can succeed.* Asking someone who often travels to attend weekly meetings may not be a good idea. Recruiting a project manager for a specific outreach event is an excellent idea. The two primary foci for youth should be following up on prospects and visitors and creating activities designed specifically for expanding your prospect list.

The follow-up component of outreach is something that should involve your students, not only adults. Students are masters of communication through a variety of media. They can talk on the phone, send email and text messages, use instant messaging, and hang around in chat rooms. Sometimes they can do all of these at once. Encourage students to find a niche. Help them to be successful and communicate to prospects by giving them the basics of what you want them to do. This may range from a "thanks for visiting" email to a phone call inviting a friend to an outreach event. Many times we assume that parents come to church with their children, but this may not be the case. They may be members elsewhere or they may be driving their children to church and then going to get coffee. Some youth visitors are at your church only because a friend invited them and was able to bring them. Adults should also be involved in this area, doing many of the same tasks. One area were adults may differ is talking to parents of prospects to learn about where the family stands in church membership and student crisis issues. Then adults can extend an invitation to students' parents as well. Two sample scripts are available at the end of this chapter.

The outreach activities component is designed to plan and implement specific activities that bring your target age group to the church for a fun, educational, non-threatening event. These events are times to invite youth back for Sunday school or worship. It is an opportunity to include your students in outreach by requiring that they bring a guest in order to be admitted. Finally, the names of guests should be recorded along with basic information (phone number, email, hobbies, church affiliation). The following are examples of these activities:

- *Scavenger Hunt.* Plan an old-fashioned scavenger hunt through town or even in the church building. Recruit parent drivers, hand out video cameras or disposable cameras, and send them on their way with a list.

- *Outing.* Encourage youth to invite guests to a preplanned special event at no cost. A Christian concert is an easy idea, as well as a local sporting event or a bowling night.

- *Exam Break Coffeehouse.* Line up local talent or rent a karaoke machine and ask a local coffeehouse to cater the event at your church. You might even ask if they will allow you to take over their shop for a few hours at the end of exams. Many students today consume coffee drinks and enjoy hanging out together.

(3) *Get organized.* After you recruit your outreach team, have an organizational meeting. At this meeting, you should develop a master calendar and an idea list. Maintain the idea list even if the idea does not fit this year's calendar. The more resources you have to pull from, the better. Determine how you will assign prospects to your follow-up

volunteers and how your volunteers will report back about their progress. Prepare your activities team with dates, promotional checklists, and action plans for their events. Encourage everyone to take part in the activities as well as the welcoming of guests at special events and Sunday school. Be aware that outreach should be fun, so build fun into your meeting.

(4) Distribute resources to the members of the team. They will need copies of the calendar, sample scripts, follow-up worksheets, and the mission statement of the outreach team.

Okay, I'm Here. Now What?

Imagine a college basketball team whose coach does a marvelous job of recruiting the nation's top talent to play basketball at his school. Now imagine that the team does a lousy job on the court. They win about half of their games but never live up to their potential. If you saw this happening, what do you think the problems would be? Most likely the coach did well getting the players there, but he failed to do a good job developing their potential. Unfortunately, churches can be guilty of this same type of treatment with their members. So much time and energy is spent on reaching out to prospects that those already there are essentially ignored. This is an awful but common mistake. Therefore, the next portion of this chapter deals with the inreach ministry of Sunday school.

In order for students to grow in their faith, they must be challenged to put it into action. Many teenagers are good at meeting new people and developing new friendships, but there are others who do a good job at keeping up with people. They effectively recognize who is missing or who may need a kind word. These students may be uncomfortable with outreach but can do a wonderful job with inreach. The needs and concerns of the students in your class need to be addressed. Why have they missed the last two weeks? What good things should the class know about? Who has lost a loved one or needs prayer for a crisis in his or her life? These are all things dealing with inreach, which is essentially the ministry to and for the students in your class.

Inreach does several things effectively. First and foremost, it establishes community by developing relationships. These relationships are student-to-student and student-to-teacher. Every young person needs quality adult relationships as well as quality peer relationships. Sunday school provides a small community in which these relationships can begin, be nurtured, and grow. Relationships are essential to developing trust, communicating the love of Christ, and earning the right to be heard. Develop these relationships by communicating care for the good and the bad happening in the lives of students.

Despite how comfortable you may be sharing prayer concerns, needs, or praises in Sunday school, students may not be as inclined to share in a group setting. Thus you may know that something is wrong with a student, but he or she will not share it in class. Through inreach ministry, you can learn about the hurts and needs of your students on an individual basis. You can at least offer them the knowledge that you are praying for them. Other students may not be as inclined to share the good things happening to them, but through this type of ministry you can recognize each individual for achievements, awards, and other special occasions.

A Peek at Inreach

Inreach requires a special person or group of people. Those special people are the F.A.C.E. of caring ministry for your Sunday school.

F:Follow-through—What good is it to be aware of someone who needs a touch if you do not follow through? Volunteers for inreach need to be capable of following through with people who need to be contacted. They also must be good at communicating needs effectively to the rest of the class. When a person in a class lost her job and communicated it as a prayer request, the class was able to make that person part of their personal and collective prayer life. They were also able to communicate concern to the individual and her family. Without this process of communication, Sunday school classes risk becoming little more than book clubs.

A:Authenticity—A genuine diamond tells a woman something that cubic zirconium probably does not. Likewise, an authentic person is able to relate and communicate with a person much more effectively than a person who is simply doing a duty. When recruiting volunteers for inreach, do not simply fill a list with warm bodies. Seek people who are concerned about others and are capable of communicating concern through words and tone. Nothing is worse than sensing that the person who called to ask about you actually does not care. Conversely, nothing is better than realizing that the person has a sincere concern for you and your needs.

C:Compassion—You probably do not want a person calling others who is going to give advice or judge someone for actions or feelings. Adults are too quick to dismiss the hurts of a student as an "insignificant issue." Consider the death of a family pet. Many adults roll their eyes at this prayer request, but if you have ever lost a family pet, then you know the deep pain this can cause. These same adults probably make mountains out of molehills in their own lives or have forgotten how significant certain issues were when they were teenagers. Encourage any volunteer, youth or adult, to act with compassion and sincerity among those needing care.

E:Empathy—Finally, there is the need for empathy, which encompasses the previous two ideals of authenticity and compassion. However, empathy takes on additional weight when doing inreach. In Paul's letter to the Corinthians (1 Cor 12), he says that when one part of the body rejoices, all parts should rejoice; when one part suffers, they all should suffer with it. In relationships, most people are good at celebrating the good things that happen to others, yet they struggle to suffer with the same people. In many cases, the suffering person may need someone to sense his or her pain, sitting quietly in support rather than needing to hear the details. A sufferer may need someone who can pray when he or she is unable to find the words to communicate with God. Sometimes we need someone who can live Romans 8:26 for us.

How-tos of Inreach

A team that guides this type of ministry should operate on two assumptions: First, meet people where they are rather than expecting them to come to you. This is similar to what was said regarding outreach. People are not likely to come and tell you everything happening in their lives, whether good or bad. As someone participating in inreach, you must be prepared to go to them. Second, many students live with issues they want to cry out about, but they are not sure where it is safe to do so. Hopefully, your student ministry provides a safe place to express deep feelings. If not, you now have a goal for inreach. For a successful inreach ministry in your youth Sunday school class, you need people willing to invest themselves and genuinely care about their fellow journeyers. The structure of this ministry might resemble the following model.

(1) *Recruit a volunteer who is the contact point for the ministry needs of the class membership.* This person should always be made aware of current needs that can be added to the general prayer list. As needs are communicated to this person, he or she can communicate them to the remainder of the class. Immediate needs may need to be handled through a series of telephone calls, while less immediate needs may be added to the prayer list on Sunday morning. Websites and emails are other good ways to communicate needs.

(2) *Develop a team of helpers who adopt a variety of tasks that will enhance the caring ministry of the class.* One person may be responsible for sending a card from the class for birthdays and anniversaries. Another may be responsible for planning social events for the class, such as parties, guys'/girls' nights out, or lunch after church at a favorite restaurant. Another may want to call every person in the class

on a monthly basis to touch base, say hello, and tell them they were prayed for that day.

Ultimately, the responsibility of inreach falls on each and every person in the class. One person can never know all of the needs, concerns, joys, and events that take place in the life of the class. When everyone is committed to the process and communicates through a central person, great community can be built and nurtured.

Saturday Caller

This idea works equally well for both inreach and outreach ministry. People are apt to remember a phone call they receive inviting them to church or communicating care for at least a day or so. With this in mind, why not make calls to students on Saturday? You may miss high school students on Saturday night, but why not call them in the middle of the day, about the time they wake up? Invite them to church the following day. Tell them you were thinking of them this week and wanted to see how their week went. Often, students have not made plans for the current day, much less the following one, so a contact may encourage them to incorporate Sunday school into their day. Students will go where they feel loved, and a phone call communicates that plainly. Here are two sample scripts for Saturday caller, one for outreach and one for inreach:

Saturday Caller for Outreach
-Hi, this is _____ from _____ Church.
-How are you doing?
-I noticed that you attended our church (or outreach event) on
        _____ (date).
-I hope you enjoyed your time with us.
-I don't want to take too much of your time, but I wanted to say thanks for
        coming and extend an invitation for you to join us tomorrow
        morning for Sunday school at _____ (time).
-Is there anything else you'd like to know about our church?
-Well, I hope to see you tomorrow. I'll be looking for you.

Saturday Caller for Inreach

-Hi, this is _____ from your Sunday school class at church.

-How are you doing?

-I missed you last Sunday and was calling to see how your week at school went.

-I thought about you a couple of times this week, so I wanted to call and let you know. I hope to see you tomorrow.

-Is there anything going on that I can pray about for you? (If so, say that you will and that you will be looking for them tomorrow.)

-(If not, say "Great, well I'll be looking for you tomorrow.")

A short phone call to parents of visiting youth can also work wonders for outreach. Here is a sample script for a phone call to a parent:

Sample Script for Adult to Parent Phone Call

-Hi, this is _____ from _____ Church.

-How are you doing?

-I am an adult volunteer at the church, and I met _____ this past week. I hope he/she enjoyed his/her time with us.

-As a parent, I like to know what my child is involved in, so I thought I would call and ask if there is anything you would like to know about our church.

-(Answer questions honestly.)

-I don't want to take too much more of your time, but I wanted to introduce myself to you. Have you attended any of our services before?

-(If so, invite them back.)

-(If not, say, "I would like to meet you in person. Please join us for church this Sunday morning. Sunday school is at _____ and worship at _____. I'll wait for a few minutes at the welcome center before Sunday school.")

-Thanks again for letting _____ join us at _____.

-I hope to see you Sunday. I'll be looking for you.

Can't reach your youth by phone? A simple but effective way is to drop them an email. Here is a sample email useful for outreach and inreach:

Sample for Youth to Youth Email

-Hi.

-It's _____ from _____ Church.

-How's it going? I thought it was cool seeing you at church (or outreach event) on _____(date). I hope you had fun. We do lots of fun stuff at church and have a good time. We have Sunday school at _____ (time) this Sunday. If you want to come, I'll pick you up or wait for you out front.

-If you want to know more about our church, check out www.mychurch.com.

-C ya soon.

Conclusion

Youth—A Challenge and a Blessing

After his last day of kindergarten, Nana asked Graham if he was happy to be done with school for the year. He cheerfully responded, "Yes!" Then, after thinking for a moment, he asked, "Nana, when will I be done with Sunday school?" Obviously, Graham is not a big fan of having to sit quietly in Sunday school and "Big Church"!

Many of our youth probably feel this way too! We have been so busy taking care of our personal ego needs to teach that we have neglected the youth learners for whom we are responsible. Teaching should motivate learners to participate with us. Teaching is not just about me as the teacher. Hopefully, through this book, you've picked up helpful insights into teaching youth learners. Hopefully, your youth learners are not ready to "be done" with youth Sunday school.

Bo shares, "a few months ago, I walked into our home office. Our college-aged daughter was home for a weekend stay. She was at the computer working on a term paper for a class. The television was on, the stereo was playing, she was talking on the phone, and about ten "instant messenger" boxes kept popping up. All this data bombarded her and she managed quite well. 'Katie,' I offered, 'you've got to turn something off in here. Your brain is going to explode!'"

Many of our youth multitask like this every day! They are capable of managing several tasks and information streams at once. Probably, you have had to find a quiet room, perhaps with a little background music, in order to concentrate on this book. Right now, I'm sitting in a crowded airport terminal, the stereo is blaring, frequent announcements are being made, cell phones are ringing, the man next to me is talking on his phone with a loud voice, and people are pushing and shoving. I'm not filtering out much of anything. We probably don't "multitask" well, but youth today are nearly experts at it.

The point is that when they come to us for learning, they can handle more than one medium at a time. Use variety in your teaching, challenge all their senses, and keep them interested in the teaching/learning experience. Youth learn differently today than we did as teenagers. Keep them interested and engaged.

One day my daughter was downstairs and was fussing about our microwave. "What's the matter with you?" I inquired. "Dad, your microwave is just too slow!" she exclaimed.

Many of our youth think similarly about our adult world. They are the instant generation. They have returned from school to empty homes and popped in a "mac and cheese" snack. They have sat for hours in front of the television visiting with "instant friends" on MTV. They have gone into chat rooms and made "virtual" relationships instantly with people all over the world. Then they come to us on Sunday morning and sit!

We must tailor our teaching to respond to the world in which our young people live. We are not suggesting that we turn our teaching into an MTV production, but rather that we teach with awareness of their world. We are more than a "geyser" of spiritual information, spewing each Sunday for an hour. We are to be in the world of our teenagers. Jesus modeled for us sensitivity to all with whom he came in contact. Jesus was always able to relate his teachings to the audience. If we are going to do more than simply survive the Sunday school hour, we also must be sensitive, aware, creative, and relevant.

One extremely busy Sunday, "Miss Angela" twisted my arm and asked me to help in the four-year-old room. What was I thinking? Yet, saying "no" has never been one of my strong points. As I watched the children exploring all sorts of things in the room, I was again reminded of the wonderful curiosity of learners. As I told them a short Bible story, one blonde cutie asked, "And that means God loves us, right?" I was amazed at her insight!

Many youth react to our teaching in much the same way. Like young children, they are curious about life. Granted, their issues are a lot more complex, but they are still into learning about God, about God's will for their lives, and about how to live obediently. Youth of today desire to grow in wisdom and in stature and in favor with God and people. Youth of today desire to learn how to love the Lord with all their heart and mind, how to love their neighbors, and how to love themselves. Our paying attention to them helps us know how to help them learn and grow. I am always amazed when a young person "gets it." Just like our little four-year-old friend, youth also have "a-ha" moments. There is nothing more exciting than seeing learning happen in the life of a learner, especially a youth learner. We love it when a young person has a "light bulb" go off in their head or heart and a truth is internalized in that mysteriously exciting moment. Wow!

Equally, there is nothing more exciting than when a youth has an insight that teaches us. In our years of working with young people, there have been times when a youth have taught us. A youth learner may have seen something in a way we had not considered. Or he/she might have experienced something we never thought about or experienced ourselves. We love it when a young person becomes the teacher for that mysteriously exciting moment. Wow!

Prepared For and Cared For!

By now, you have read this mantra on many of these pages. You know that preparation is more than simply getting a lesson ready. You've learned that caring for youth is more than simply standing to deliver each Sunday.

Youth are special people. Many think youth are the church of tomorrow. We challenge you to see that youth are the church of today too! The culture in which they live is certainly different from when you and I grew up. The way they learn, the way they relate, the things they do for fun—all of these events have changed since the good old fifties, sixties, seventies, and eighties.

Youth learn today from all sorts of places, from some reliable teachers and some not so reliable teachers. We want youth to be motivated to come to Sunday school. This will only happen as they feel prepared for and cared for.

Information and Transformation

The minister worked with youth for many years. She programmed activities. She encouraged teenagers to come; she went to their ball-games and concerts; she ate in their high school lunchrooms. She went on lock-ins; she went on retreats; she did everything she knew to do to help them grow in wisdom and stature, and in favor with God and people (see Luke 2:52).

During a training session one weekend, the trainer said to her learning group, "I know you know how to program for your youth. But what are you doing to make disciples?"

This question impacted the youth minister. For all the years she had been "doing," she had forgotten about "being"! She was so busy teaching facts and principles that she overlooked the need for helping the youth apply what she taught them.

Youth learners need to know more than Bible facts. They need to know how to apply Bible truths. Youth learners need to wrestle with Bible truths and discover applications for these in their daily living. They need to have their faith based on solid foundations as they go out into their youth worlds and grow into their adult worlds.

Adulthood is a challenging place. As youth approach adulthood and begin making adult choices, they need a strong faith base from which to work. I've worked with too many adults who never received good Bible teaching. Their worlds were wrecked by too many negative influences. They never knew how to claim Christ and live bravely. Today's youth face overwhelming issues. We cannot teach simply to give out information. We must teach with intentionality to lead youth into transformation.

In several of Paul's writings, he gives the Trinitarian reference to having been saved, now being saved, and one day being fully saved. Paul is not only talking about his salvation experience. Paul is talking about everyday growth. Paul also speaks to us about being a new creation in Christ. This newness is not a one-time happening. It is an everyday renewal.

We know too many adults who were "saved" at a young age and have never grown past that initial salvation experience. We cannot let youth rest on their initial salvation. We must teach them and lead them and model for them healthy Christian faith. As we do, we may one day be able to say with Paul, "I have fought a good fight, I have finished [my] course, I have kept the faith" (2 Tim 4:7).

Let us teach while still learning. Let us lead without being demanding. Let us care deeply without holding too tightly. Mostly, let us love, O Lord, let us love!

101 Creative Teaching Ideas

Using Art

(1) *Three-dimensional visuals.* Create objects and lesson helps usin-boxes, balls, blocks, etc.

(2) *Large sheets of paper and markers.* Trace bodies, present answers, ask questions, doodle, make pictures, etc.

(3) *Blank paper pictures/doodles.* Give students a blank piece of paper and have them draw a picture about the lesson. Or they can doodle and be creative.

(4) *Paper, scissors, and glue.* Give youth freedom to express themselves and what they interpret through these artistic mediums.

(5) *Cartoon "speech bubbles."* Provide the biblical passage and a sheet with speech bubbles. Youth fill in dialogue as it is being read.

(6) *Collage.* Make a poster using magazine pictures, yarn, and other objects or pictures.

(7) *Create cartoons.* Provide the biblical passage, paper, and pens. Youth create stick drawings and create a cartoon based on what they think the Bible lesson is about.

(8) *Exhibits/displays.* Youth create a learning center based on the lesson. The exhibit or display can be used for the following weeks.

(9) *Graffiti wall.* Give youth free reign to write on the chalkboard or sheets of paper on the wall.

(10) *Greeting cards.* Make greeting cards to emphasize the main point or idea from the lesson.

(11) *Masks.* Youth draw faces that express their emotions, and then wear the masks and help the class discuss what they portray.

(12) *Mouthless faces.* Provide a sheet with mouthless faces. As the Scripture is read, ask youth to complete the faces with the emotions they feel as they hear the passage.

(13) *Play with Play-Doh!* Distribute it for creative molding as the story or passage is read. The creations can lead to wonderful discussions.

(14) *Stick figures.* Recreate the story or lesson using stick figures so that even "non-artistic" youth can participate.

(15) *Video.* Create music or drama videos from the lesson. Add sections each week to create a miniseries or full-length presentation.

Using Drama

(16) *Act without words—mime.* Read the Scripture and allow youth time to create actions to what you read.

(17) *Charades.* Act out the lesson or the story using motions without words. Have the rest of the class guess what the lesson or story is.

(18) *Dialogue.* Let the dialogue of two (or more) characters carry the lesson. Create the dialogue based on the lesson—reactions to an event, relationships, etc.; or use the text as it is written.

(19) *Divine conversation.* Create a conversation between God and humanity based on the lesson or story.

(20) *Drama.* Tell them the story and give youth time to prepare a dramatic interpretation with words, actions, and props if available.

(21) *Finish the story.* For biblical stories without an ending, ask your students to write their own ending and act it out.

(22) *Human map.* Use bodies to create a city or the landscape. Then use actors to tell the story.

(23) *Monologue.* One-person skit in which a student or teacher pretends to be a biblical character.

(24) *Present-day Bible.* "Rewrite" the lesson and act it out in a present-day setting.

(25) *Puppets.* If your church has puppets, use them to tell the story. If not, make simple puppets and use them to tell the story. Take the "show" to a children's Sunday school class.

(26) *Role-playing.* Create scenarios based on the lesson and give to individuals or small groups to come up with a solution.

(27) *Spontaneous melodrama.* Designate a reader and select "actors" to do what the story says. Allow freedom for humor and stretching the event (but not the truth).

(28) *Talk show interview.* Before Sunday, assign roles to an interviewer and the biblical character to be interviewed. They can tell the story or the truth through this format.

(29) *Trial.* Put biblical figures "on trial" with students serving as judge/jury.

(30) *TV show.* Use a current TV show as the basis for teaching the lesson. Substitute the TV characters or scenarios with the biblical characters or scenarios.

Using Music

(31) *Circular song.* Pick a tune familiar to everyone and have each person write one line of the lyrics as the song is passed around the circle.

(32) *Create a song.* Break into smaller groups and have each group create a song using the same tune.

(33) *Group singing.* Sing songs that support the lesson.

(34) *Lyric study.* Provide lyrics and discuss those in light of the Bible study.

(35) *Musical drama.* Using only music in the background, act out the story or lesson.

(36) *Musical guess.* Tape segments of several songs that relate to the lesson. Ask your students to guess the title of the song and how it applies to the lesson.

(37) *Musical motion.* Listen closely to a song and then have the class move their bodies the way the music makes them feel.

(38) *"Pop" music.* Find contemporary songs to help teach the lessons. Songs can help teach a lesson with both their positive message and their negative message. Encourage your class to help identify songs that will help with an upcoming lesson.

(39) *Sounds.* Record sounds that relate to the lesson and play them at appropriate points throughout the study.

(40) *Use a hymnal.* Bring in hymnals to reinforce the Bible lesson. Encourage the youth to find songs that relate to the truth in the lesson.

Using Paper and Pens

(41) *Acrostics.* Using one word from the lesson, ask the students to define the lesson or truth using the letters from that one word. For example:

For me to share with others
Always an option in difficult times
I struggle putting this into practice
Trusting in things not seen
Helps when there is doubt

(42) *Biography.* When studying a specific character, have students write as much as they know about the person to create a biography. Keep all biographies on file in the classroom to refer to later.

(43) *Book title.* Create a title for a book someone might write about the theme presented in the lesson.

(44) *Create a crossword puzzle.* Students take the lesson and main ideas and create a crossword puzzle for a children's Sunday school class.

(45) *Encyclopedia entry.* Students write an entry that will be included in the new biblical encyclopedia.

(46) *Fishbowl a biblical truth or verse.* After reading a story, passage, or verse, invite the class to write down one question or thought about what they heard. Gather all the questions and go through them as a group, answering or discussing them.

(47) *Letter writing.* Students write letters to the character of the story or the author of the book.

(48) *Mail.* Introduce the lesson with a card or letter sent earlier in the week.

(49) *Note-taking.* Encourage students to take notes using their neighbors' backs while sitting in a circle.

(50) *Paraphrase.* Rewrite the passage or story in your own words.

(51) *Prayers.* Give each student time to reflect and compose his or her own prayer based on the lesson, truth, or need from the Scripture.

(52) *Five-line Poems.* Reflect on the passage and write a five-line poem.
- First line: title
- Second line: two words of explanation
- Third line: three words to tell what the title does
- Fourth line: four words to tell how you feel about the title
- Fifth line: one word that means the same as the title

(53) *Reflection journal.* Provide a three-ring notebook to keep in the classroom. Ask students to record their thoughts or ideas each time a story or passage is read. This can be helpful to review and chart the "growth" of the class.

(54) *Reverse paraphrase.* Write the "opposite" of what the Scripture says. For example, "The Lord is my shepherd, I shall not want" might be "The Lord is not my shepherd. Actually, he doesn't know where I am. I am in constant need." This can be a wonderful exercise to study the actual truth of a passage.

(55) *Rewrite Paul's letters for today.* What words would Paul use today? How would Paul address the problems at your church? How would Paul praise you for keeping the faith?

(56) *Scrambled story.* Separate each sentence in the story. The group must put the story back together in the proper order.

(57) *Test.* Create a test from the lesson and give prizes for correct answers.

(58) *Trademarks or logos.* Create a trademark or logo based on the biblical truth from the lesson.

(59) *Want ads.* Students write a want ad for the author, text, or character in the story.

(60) *Web page design.* Students create (on paper) a web site that explains the biblical truth or story. Encourage them to create different pages, links, graphics, etc.

(61) *Word scramble.* Scramble the letters of the main word or grouping of words. Ask students to rearrange them in correct order.

(62) *Word study.* Give each small group a word to examine in the lesson.

(63) *Youth-written test.* After the lesson, have the students write a test to give to each other.

Using Words

(64) *Being there.* Through the use of questions and suggestions, encourage the class the place themselves in the scenario.

(65) *Brainstorming.* Present an idea, passage, or truth and then let the youth brainstorm about it. Record their answers for later reference.

(66) *Create a game show.* Ask questions and answers and reward correct responses with an "X" or "O" on a big tic-tac-toe grid. Keep points. Create Sunday school Jeopardy—"I'll take 'Biblical Boats' for $500!"

(67) *Debate.* Form two groups and have one group support the truth and one group speak against the truth. Formalize the debate so each group gets equal time to present their case. Discuss the experience.

(68) *Different translations.* Have the students read from different Bible translations and discuss the differences and similarities.

(69) *The hook—"Well, what are you doing about it?"* Ask this question after reading a passage or story. It is wonderful for discussion and going deeper with the study.

(70) *I remember.* Ask the class to retell the story before it is read. Discuss what they remembered and what they forgot.

(71) *Reteaching.* Invite a children's Sunday school class to share the lesson. Have the students share the Sunday school lesson with a children's class. The youth can help explain, help with crafts, help with singing, etc. Make sure the lesson will work for children.

(72) *Invite an outside teacher.* Bring in an adult from another part of the church to teach or share a personal experience that applies to the lesson being taught.

(73) *Newscast.* Present the story in the form of a news show. One teacher can tell what happened and others can interview students for their reactions.

(74) *Open-ended statements or questions.* These move away from "yes or no" answers and allow the youth to share deeper answers. For example, "If I were Noah when God told me to build an ark, I . . . ."

(75) *"Operator."* Whisper the truth or verse to one student. That person whispers to the person next to them, who whispers to the person next to them, etc. Finally, the last person gets the message.

(76) *Storytelling.* Find a children's book or story that relates to the lesson and read it.

(77) *Teach it wrong.* Intentionally insert incorrect information into a story or lesson. Your "error" will help students pay attention as they point out your mistakes. Tell them before you begin that you plan on "messing up."

(78) *Testimony.* Include a personal testimony to enhance the lesson.

(79) *Word association.* You say one word, and the students respond with the first word that pops into their heads. Talk about it.

(80) *You are the learner; they are the teacher.* Give the class the Bible passage and time, and then let them present to you their lesson plan.

Using Visuals

(81) *Bulletin board or collage.* Decorate the bulletin board to point out the main ideas in the lesson.

(82) *Small groups.* Form groups of three to five for questions and answers and discussion. Have them report back to the larger group.

(83) *Go outside.* Jesus taught outside—you can, too. Make sure you pick a pretty day!

(84) *Family Sunday school.* This is not a discipline method. Invite the parents of your class to come and join the youth for a combined Sunday school lesson. Make sure the lesson plan is interactive and not lecture-based.

(85) *Maps.* Biblical maps next to contemporary maps help the youth visualize the actual area where events took place.

(86) *Masterpieces.* Use works of art from the "masters " to introduce the lesson. Many masterpieces can teach an entire lesson. Most can be found in some form on the Internet.

(87) *Photography.* Before Sunday, take pictures that relate to the lesson and get them developed.

(88) *Progressive lesson.* Begin the lesson in one room or area of the church and continue to move to different locations as the "movement" of the lesson changes.

(89) *Rearrange the room.* Keep the education space fresh by rearranging the set-up in the room. The youth will appreciate the change, even if it is small.

(90) *Technology.* Bring in a VCR/DVD player and TV and play an excerpt from a television show or movie. Use appropriate material to help make the lesson or truth more applicable.

(91) *Time line.* Create a time line with cord, 3-x-5-inch cards, and clothespins. As an event is taught, add it to the time line. This will help the youth grasp the sequence of events.

(92) *Toss a beanbag or ball.* Begin a question session with a small object that can be safely tossed. Whoever catches the beanbag or ball must attempt to answer the question or add to the conversation. Then they choose who answers next by tossing that person the beanbag or ball.

(93) *Tour the church.* For lessons that deal with specific events in the life of the church—baptism, communion, etc.—leave the classroom and go to where the action takes place.

(94) *Use old Sunday school packet pictures.* Borrow from the children's ministry. Use these to help bring a visual image to the lesson.

Other Treasures

(95) *Discussion.* This method is used too often, but it is effective when students go beyond the "yes" and "no" answers.

(96) *Lecture.* Only use when the students are awake and motivated. Use it in conjunction with other ideas.

(97) *Memorization.* Use memorization to complement the lesson, not as an end unto itself.

(98) *Newspaper articles.* Bring in a current newspaper article that complements the lesson.

(99) *Questions from students.* Have the class write their own questions about the lesson. Then have them answer each other's questions.

(100) *Research and discovery.* Provide commentaries, Bible dictionaries, and Bible encyclopedias from your church library to encourage in-class research during the lesson.

(101) *Silent reading.* Give a certain amount of time for each youth to read silently—at his or her own pace.

Resources for Surviving and Thriving with Youth

Books

Barna, George. *Real Teens: A Contemporary Snapshot of Youth Culture.* Ventura CA: Gospel Light, 2001.

Bass, Dorothy C., and Don C. Richter. *Way to Live: Christian Practices for Teens.* Nashville: Upper Room Books, 2002.

Dean, Kenda Creasy, and Ron Foster. *The God Bearing Life: The Art of Soul Tending for Youth Ministry.* Nashville: Upper Room Books, 1998.

Dean, Kenda Creasy, Chap Clark, and Dave Rahn, editors. *Starting Right: Thinking Theologically About Youth Ministry.* Grand Rapids MI: Zondervan Publishing House, 2001.

McLaren, Brian. *The Church on the Other Side.* Grand Rapids MI: Zondervan Publishing House, 2003.

McNabb, Bill, and Steven Mabry. *Teaching the Bible Creatively.* Grand Rapids MI: Zondervan Publishing House, 1990.

Mueller, Walt. *Understanding Today's Youth Culture.* Wheaton IL: Tyndale House Publishers, Inc., 1999.

Murray, Dick. *Teaching the Bible to Adults and Youth.* Nashville: Abingdon Press, 1987.

Prosser, Bo, et al. *Building Blocks for Sunday School Growth.* Macon GA: Smyth & Helwys Publishing, 2002.

Strommen, Merton, and A. Irene Strommen. *Five Cries of Parents.* Minneapolis: Augsburg Youth and Family Institute, 1993.

Strommen, Merton. *Five Cries of Youth*. San Francisco: HarperCollins
    Publishers, 1993.
Sweet, Leonard, et al. *Church in Emerging Culture: Five Perspectives*.
    Grand Rapids MI: Zondervan Publishing House, 2003.

Websites

American Academy of Child and Adolescent Psychiatry
http://www.aacap.org
Created by the American Academy of Child and Adolescent
Psychiatry, this site is loaded with information on child and adolescent
psychiatry, fact sheets for parents and caregivers, AACAP membership,
current research, practice guidelines, managed care information,
awards and fellowship descriptions, meeting information, and much
more.

Antithesis
www.antithesis.com
This site offers info and cultural analysis from a thoughtful Christian
perspective in response to the challenges of thinking, living, and
understanding that characterize our postmodern age.

Barna Research Group, Ltd.
www.barna.org
Barna Research Group, Ltd. (BRG) is a full-service marketing research
company located in Ventura, California. BRG has been providing
information and analysis regarding cultural trends and the Christian
church since 1984. The company's vision is to provide organizations
with current, accurate, and reliable information in bite-sized
pieces and at affordable prices, to help facilitate effective and strategic
decision-making.

The Center for Parent/Youth Understanding
www.cpyu.org
The Center for Parent/Youth Understanding is a nonprofit organization committed to building strong families by serving to bridge the
cultural-generational gap between parents and teenagers. At a time
when an already confusing youth culture is changing quickly, CPYU
helps parents, youth workers, educators, and others understand
teenagers and their culture so that they will be better equipped to help
children and teens navigate the challenging world of adolescence.

Dick Staub—Culture Watch
www.DickStaub.com
Radio host and writer Dick Staub hosts this site that features movie,
music, book, and news reviews where "belief meets real life." Dick
believes that by listening to popular culture, one can hear and understand issues of importance to today's seeker and become literate in the
"vocabulary" most useful in communicating beliefs.

The Gospel and Our Culture Network
http://www.gocn.org
This site is helpful for those desiring to minister effectively in our current postmodern context. It brings together a wide variety of churches
and organizations working together on the frontier of the missionary
field.

Great Transitions
http://www.carnegie.org/sub/pubs/reports/great_transitions/gr_intro.
html
This online report represents the culmination of the Carnegie Council
on Adolescent Development's ten years of research on the adolescent
experience in modern culture. The site contains a synthesis of "the best
available knowledge and wisdom about adolescence in America."

www.hollywoodjesus.com
This site helps us explore the deeper, more profound meanings behind film, music, and pop culture.

The Institute for Youth Development
http://www.youthdevelopment.org
IYD is a non-partisan, non-profit organization promoting a comprehensive risk avoidance message to youth for harmful risk behaviors that are linked: alcohol, drugs, sex, tobacco, and violence. The site is designed for professionals, parents, and teens.

Junior High Pastor.com
http://wwwjuniorhighpastor.com
This site exists to equip junior high youth workers for the twenty-first century. It includes reviews, resources, and discussion of matters related to junior high ministry.

Mars Hill Forum
http://www.marshillforum.org
Mars Hill Forum exists to reveal Christ amid our current postmodern culture. The site includes journal articles and other information designed to train people to be competent in the study of the Scriptures, the culture, and human soul. This thoughtful site strives to address the needs of a rapidly changing culture.

MethodX
www.methodx.org
Developed by the Upper Room Publishers, MethodX (the way of Christ) is an online Christian community where young adults (college to thirties) can identify and explore their relationships with God and with others.

Ministry and Media
www.ministryandmedia.com
Ministry and Media assists you in discovering practical and effective ways to use popular media in your ministry. Biblical discussion starters based on videos, the latest CDs, breaking news, and the movies playing at your local theaters are added every week. You will find the tools to impact youth culture with the gospel of Jesus Christ. Relevance to culture is a necessity, not an option.

Neos Cosmos
www.neoscosmos.com
Neos Cosmos serves as the homepage for youth workers who want to engage, interpret, and better understand the world of their youth, with the ultimate goal of equipping a generation to be able to springboard off pop culture chats into spiritual conversations about timeless truths.

The Princeton Theological Seminary Institute for Youth Ministry
www.ptsem.edu/iym
The Institute for Youth Ministry's program emphasizes theological education for people in ministry with youth. "The Institute" collaborates with seminaries, church leaders, congregations, communities, and adolescents to promote the strategic importance and practice of ministry with young people from early adolescence through college age.

RELEVANT Magazine
www.relevantmagazine.com
RELEVANT has both a print magazine and an online magazine, each with its own content. Operated by a group of Gen X Christians, RELEVANT examines God, life, and progressive culture. Topics discussed include faith, career, relationships, music, and the culture at large, all from an intelligent and fresh Christian perspective. They also offer a great email newsletter.

The Search Institute
www.search-institute.org
Search Institute is an independent nonprofit organization whose mission is to provide leadership, knowledge, and resources to promote healthy children, youth, and communities. To accomplish this mission, the institute generates and communicates new knowledge and brings together community, state, and national leaders. The Search Institute is teaching developmental assets to make youth good Christians and good citizens.

Smyth & Helwys Publishing
www.helwys.com
Smyth & Helwys is a free press that reports to no denominational or outside groups in their work. Serving only churches, this freedom allows the company to create resources that are creative, relevant, and fresh. Their focus is quality Bible study. For youth and youth workers, they offer *Intersection*, a youth Sunday school curriculum; a study on calling called *The Choice* (related to the Samuel Project); and online resources.

The Source for Youth Ministry
www.thesourcefym.com
The mission of The Source for Youth Ministry is to reach twenty-first century youth with the life-changing message of Jesus Christ, develop student and adult youth leaders with effective ministry skills, and provide cutting-edge youth ministry tools and resources.

Understanding Your Teenager
http://www.uyt.com
Founded by youth ministry guru Wayne Rice, the goal of Understanding Your Teenager is to help teenagers by helping their parents. Research has proven that teenagers are more likely to succeed in life if their parents stay involved in their lives—all the way through adolescence. The organization seeks to help parents understand their kids better and stay connected.

Visual Reality
www.visualrealityonline.com
Visual Reality provides a video illustration subscription to youth workers for use in Bible studies, Sunday school lessons, and messages. Wherever students and Scripture intersect, their illustrations will help you communicate the truth of the Bible in a way to which students can relate.

Y-generation.com
http://www.y-generation.com
Billed as "the premiere y-gen info site," this one "is dedicated to providing information and services to the youth of the world." It is loaded with news, gossip, interviews, teen forums, entertainment news, sound and video clips, etc.

YouthPastor.com
www.youthpastor.com
YouthPastor.com was founded in 1997 to create the most comprehensive youth ministry network and online free resource for youth pastors. Their focus is dedicated to the youth pastor, designing resources and services that are not typically available from the church denominations and Christian curriculum publishing services. Instead, their services complement the offerings of specialized ministries and curriculum publishers.

Youth Specialties
www.youthspecialties.com
For more than thirty years, Youth Specialties has worked alongside Christian youth workers of nearly every denomination and youth-serving organization. They seek to help youth ministers and youth volunteers with all levels of experience.